The Black Attaché

**CALUMET
EDITIONS**

Minneapolis

First Edition January 2023

The Black Attaché: Vignettes from a Life
Copyright © 2023 by Jatinder Kaur Cheema
All rights reserved.

Printed in the United States of America.
10 9 8 7 6 5 4 3 2 1
ISBN: 978-1-960250-80-3

Cover and book design by Gary Lindberg

The Black Attaché

Vignettes from a Life

JK Cheema

CALUMET EDITIONS

Minneapolis

Even in the darkest moments, I always believed that things would work out and never gave up hope, as my mother taught me to do. I dedicate this book to my mother, Raminder Kaur. And to all the women in my family and the world.

Author's Note

This is a memoir—my memories as I remember them. It is not a complete story of my life, nor does it cover all aspects of my personal and or professional life. In this book, I capture some vignettes from different places and events. There are many more places and friends that I want to write about. They are not covered here, not because of their lack of significance in my life, but because I had to start somewhere. This book is the first step in sharing some of my life with the readers. I hope to do more.

Some names and characteristics have been changed to protect privacy. Some events have been compressed or elaborated and some dialogue recreated as I thought I remembered them. I recognize that others' memories of the events described in this book may be different than my own. I have done my best to tell my story as I remember it best.

Also by the Author

*As I Remember – The Life History of
Raminder Kaur Cheema*

Table of Contents

Sketch by the author's niece, Sukhmani

The Black Attaché

Once upon a time, many years ago, I bought a rectangular black attaché. It has been my trusted companion since 1985. I bought it when I was living in Washington, DC, and was preparing to move to Bangladesh for my first international job. I bought it not because it was practical. I bought it because it looked cool. Airline pilots were carrying such attachés. Over the years, I covered it with airline and hotel stickers from my travels. By 1999, its leather had worn out at the sides, and I retired it. I replaced it with a lighter briefcase and one that was more in fashion, like a tote bag. Not wanting to part with it, I started to store letters, postcards, diaries, and handwritten notes in it.

The black attaché traveled with me to Asia, Africa, Central Asia, Afghanistan, Armenia and many more places during my career, first as a development consultant with international organizations and then as a diplomat Foreign Service Officer with the United States Agency for International Development (USAID). When I stopped using the attaché as a carry-on, it became "unaccompanied baggage" to be shipped with the rest of my household effects as I moved to a new assignment in a new country every couple of years. I imagined a day when I would want to open it and go through its contents and relive my memories.

The heavier and fuller the black attaché got, the more clueless I became about organizing its contents. I could not leave it behind, even when it could hold no more diaries or notes. The fear that something might happen to me in some far-off place increased my need to have my black attaché close to me.

My black attaché and I retired and moved to Madison in 2012, with its contents still undisturbed. I could not bring myself to buy a bigger case and transfer the diaries and papers. I feared any such movement might disturb the writings and possibly lose some of the meaning. I stored it in the closet along with old pictures and other pieces of paper that I wanted to keep forever.

In 2018, I took a memoir writing class and reading Joan Didion's essay "On Keeping a Notebook," I thought of my black attaché.

The article inspired me to tackle the contents of the attaché, but I wanted to wait for a perfect day. A month or two and then another year passed.

Then, one day, a sunless, cloudy, and cold Wisconsin day in February of 2019, I went to the storage closet to look for something. I do not remember what, when my gaze fell on the black attaché. I paused; I felt a sudden urge to touch it. Maybe this is the day, I thought.

I brought it out of the storage room and set it on the table made from old-growth white pine boards, sixteen inches wide and one-inch-thick, that came from the south shore of Lake Superior. The friend who made it calls it a "shroud of Turin" because if you look closely at the two matching boards, you can imagine a face peering out at you. A perfect place to lay out my memories, I thought. I made coffee. I slowly dialed the combination to unlock the case and pulled on the handle. The latch clicked open. There, right in front of me, safe and sound, lay years of my life: letters, postcards, loose pieces of paper, and a row of notebooks and diaries methodically placed in the tight space.

I reached in and pulled out the first diary. I remembered it well. The leather cover smelled old and dusty and had darkened from a light rich brown to nearly black. I remembered the day I bought it in Florence, at a shop on one of the narrow streets near Piazza del Duomo, during a trip in 2001. It was late in the evening, and I was on my way back to our hotel after a long day of sightseeing. I saw this softly lit window decorated with all colors of diaries and shades of paper. I had to enter. Without opening the diary, I gently placed it on the table. I then reached in and pulled out a notebook bound in a soft red and blue handmade material, tied with a bright yellow ribbon. The sheets were made from bark. I bought the notebook in the Bada Bazaar in Udaipur in 1987, one of the oldest markets in the city. On a narrow pedestrian street, tiny and large stores sell silver, silks, leather, and local artwork, which reflects the colors of the region. A landscape of bright yellows, reds, greens, and blues displayed on buildings and on peoples' clothes surrounds you as you walk from store to store, looking for antiques and Rajasthani specialties. I saw a small stationary store tucked in between a jewelry shop and an artist's studio with a sign showing paper goods in a local language that I could not read.

Looking deeper into the attaché, I was drawn to another small brownish diary with a hard paper cover with uneven edges. I took it out and noted the imprint of an Egyptian queen inside the cover. A papyrus-made diary, which I had bought in 1975 while walking around Khan el-Khalili, a famous souk in the historic part of Cairo, Egypt. I opened it. There were few entries. The paper was extremely thin, and from the few entries, it appeared that the paper was torn in places, maybe the reason I stopped writing in it. I held the diary for a few minutes and was transformed to the wonderful soft lights and sounds of the Cairo souk, which seemed so magical to me then, especially the glasswork and ceramics reflected in the windows in their brilliant colors. When I returned to Cairo in 2011, I was disappointed by how commercialized the bazaar had become. It had larger stores and more Chinese and factory-made goods, losing some of the charm of the old bazaar.

I took the remaining memories out and stacked them on the table. I randomly picked up some pieces of paper and saw incomplete thoughts scribbled on them. After going through many notes, I wondered why I had saved them.

And then, I found a folded letter addressed to me in my mother's handwriting, dated September 17, 1983. I received it in late

October. It was a one-page letter written on an eight by eleven yellow legal pad. In 1983, I was living in Georgetown, Washington, DC, on K Street in a two-story, two-bedroom historic house that I shared with a friend. I had just started my first full-time job after completing my studies in Ann Arbor. My mom was living in New Delhi, India. At the beginning of the letter, she made a reference to a letter that I had sent her mentioning the death of a friend and how his wife was having a hard time. My letter must have stuck a chord as her letter expressed her grief over the loss of my dad, who had died earlier in 1982. She wrote about being sad. "Living without your daddy is difficult, life is extremely hard, but what to do. You must take life as it comes. I will pull through, don't worry," she wrote. She goes on to give me news of my brother and the rest of the family in a few short sentences and ends with, "I will write you again later today. I am a little depressed."

I jolted out of my chair. I realized that this was the first time since my father's death that she expressed sadness and used the word "depressed." I do not remember how I responded to her letter. Reading it again, I was upset at myself for having boxed it away and forgotten about it. It was one of the rare times that she had expressed any emotions to me about his death and her own feelings. This letter was a rare insight into the side of my mom that no one had seen. After Dad's death, stoic as a rock, we relied on her to get us through the years that followed. Tears started to swell in my eyes. She had been depressed—who had been there to help her? Did anyone know? What did I do? I stopped going through the black attaché. I went for a long walk on the dreary cold winter day, hoping I had been of some help to her in her moment of need, but then I remembered that I did not respond. Letters in those days took months to reach India from the US, and I knew that by the time my letter reached her, Mom would have forgotten about what she wrote in her letter. I never mentioned the letter to her.

I waited a week before I returned to the black attaché. I saw folded blue aerogrammes with the Mahatma Gandhi stamps on them. They were from my nieces and written between 1992 and 1997. I laid them on the table in chronological order by year. Both of my nieces were at a boarding school in the Himalayas during that time. The youngest was nine years old in 1992. I sat down on a chair next to the table and started reading the letters.

Each letter started with "Hello Phui (Punjabi word for your dad's sister). Every inch of the aerogramme was filled with news of the school, what time they wake up, what they did that day, how they are doing at school. Any empty space was used to draw faces and other funny sketches. And there were complaints about the school and the hard work. All the letters ended with "When are you coming to India? I miss you, waiting for your letter." I did wonder if writing a letter was a weekly assignment but was touched by the thought that they had thought of me. Reading their letters, I felt their love all these years later. I straightened the aerograms as the creases were tearing them in some places. I put them in a file folder for safety. I knew that I would read them again.

There were also postcards scattered around in the black leather attaché. The postcard images made the places so alluring and fascinating. I found one postcard from my dad on which he wrote, "I am so proud of you, well done. Love, Dad." The postmark read Bangkok, but the date was illegible. He was working for the World Bank in 1978, and I was finishing my PhD in Ann Arbor. Reading the postcard made me happy. He was always incredibly supportive of what I wanted to do and be. The postcard was an affirmation of his support, but he had never said it to me in person. I was glad that I had saved the postcard.

By the end of March, I had emptied the black attaché and made folders for letters and notes and laid them on the table. Looking at the stacks, I was reminded of Joan Didion's essay in which she points out that notes are to help us keep in touch with the past and the present. "And, I suppose, keeping in touch is what notebooks are all about," she wrote.

I put the newly organized diaries, letters, handwritten pieces, and postcards back in the black attaché. I had started my own journey to find out what my notes and diaries would tell me about my past and present. As I write my memoir, I go to the black attaché, reach out for a diary, a letter, or a postcard for context, and gently move my hand across the rest of the memory treasures for assurance and for inspiration.

The Village House

One of my earliest memories is of a visit to my grandparents' village home in Wadhai Cheema, in Punjab when India and Pakistan were still one country. Wadhai Cheema was a farming village where Muslims and Sikhs had lived together for generations. Most everyone living in the village, no matter what religion, shared the last name Cheema. Wadhai Cheema is also spelled as Badhai Cheema by some family members. There are number of villages now with the last name Cheema in Punjab India and Punjab Pakistan, but with different first names.

When we visited my grandparents during the summer, we traveled by train. I loved the train rides. The rhythmic sound of the metal wheels on the rails mesmerized me. The smell and the feel of soot from the coal-burning engine on my face as I sat close to the steel bars on the window made me feel alive.

I would laugh as the trees and houses swept past in the fleeting air.

My favorite part of the journey was our breakfast on the train. At the first stop, my mother would order our breakfast. Usually, a boy wearing a brown shirt and pants, who looked older than he was, took our order of tea, milk, toast, chapattis, and boiled eggs. Magically, at the next stop, our breakfast, hot and fresh, was delivered. I was always fascinated by the mystery of how our breakfast ordered at one train stop appeared at the next, all hot and freshly made.

My other favorite parts of the train ride were the stops at the larger railway stations. As soon as the train started to slow down to enter a railway station, a bazaar would open outside my window. Hawkers with baskets on their heads walked back and forth, selling hot tea, biscuits, fruits, newspapers, and toys if they spotted a child. I wanted it all. Five hours later, we would arrive at a small brick structure called "the Rayia Station," surrounded by wheat fields.

I remember one visit when the train came to a stop, and a flood of red-turbaned porters entered the compartment to help carry the luggage. My mother held my sister in one of her arms and me by the hand, and we descended to the platform. Our suitcases were precariously loaded on top of one of the red-turbaned porters whom we followed out of the station. As we exited the station, I saw three large brown horses and a bearded man with a large turban wound around and over his head leading the horses toward us. The bearded man folded his hand and greeted my mother with "Sat Sri Akal," the Sikh greeting.

I recognized Inder Singh from my previous visit. I clapped my hands as he reached down and affectionately patted my head. Everyone was always patting children on their heads. Most times, I hated it, but I did not mind now since I liked Inder Singh. He worked for my grandfather and took me for bike rides through the wheat fields.

The porter placed the luggage on one horse and tightly strapped the suitcases. Inder Singh helped my mother mount the second horse. My mother reached down to take my sister and held her tightly with one hand and the reins with the other. Then it was my turn. I looked at the big horse. I knew that I was not getting on that horse. My mother assured me that I would be fine. She reminded me that I had ridden on the horse with Inder Singh the previous summer. The previous summer was a long time ago. I insisted upon walking.

The shadows from the sun had deepened to orange. Still, there was enough summer light, but it would be dark soon.

"We need to move," I heard my mom say.

Suddenly, I felt Inder Singh's strong arms lifting me, and with one big swing, he deposited me on the saddle. He climbed up behind me, holding me safely. I started screaming. I complained all the way, insisting that I wanted to walk through the fields. I did not want anyone to know that I was afraid.

We arrived at the entrance of the village as the sky was turning to a hazy pink. Herds of cattle were returning to the village after grazing all day in the fields. The old wood and brass bells around their necks made rhythmic sounds with each step. Young boys with small sticks in their hands guided the cattle with softly encouraging sounds towards their homes for the night, leaving behind a track of dust and a strong earthy smell.

At the outskirts of the village, our convoy of three horses moved through a muddy and narrow path and stopped in front of a fort-like wooden gate. The gate opened. I saw my grandfather, with his long loose beard, coming out to greet us. He wore a white turban and the traditional kurta pajama outfit that men wear in rural Punjab.

The house was huge, with a square courtyard in the middle and a verandah all around. The rooms had high ceilings with stained glass windows. I remember on one side of the courtyard there were the living quarters: on the second, the kitchen area and the storage rooms for grain and household items. Beyond that was the shed for the cows, horses, goats and hens. It was the busiest part of the house. The animals needed attention all the time. There was a long room on the side of the entrance for visitors who came to see my grandfather, who was the village administrative head, a position sometimes designated by lineage and sometimes by the government.

My favorite room in the house was the one in which I slept. It had a large bed on which my mom, my sister and I slept together. There was a stained-glass window over a large wooden door through which the sunlight created wonderful colors and patterns across my room in the morning. I anxiously waited for the sun to shine every morning. I would lie there for hours playing games with the colors and the shadows creating characters and making stories. I tried to catch the red and blues until the sun moved away.

In the outside visitor's room, farmers and workers who came to see my grandfather would sit on the wooden platform-like beds strung with jute or straw and covered with colorful bedspreads. Tea and water were served all day. Sometimes my grandfather would let me sit with him. They would talk about local politics, the rains, the crops, and their financial problems. I liked listening to them and felt grown up sitting beside him. Some days, they all sat under a huge banyan tree that stood a little further from the house; I was not supposed to go there, but I would sneak up when no one was looking. I wanted to know when the monsoons were coming or if we would have sugarcane and mangoes that summer. I wanted to be part of their conversation.

Inside the house, my grandmother's sitting space was readied every morning, much like my grandfather, for her to receive visitors, mostly women, wearing salwar kameez, the Punjabi outfit. A large colorful scarf called a chunni (north Indian scarf worn mostly in Punjab) covered their heads. Some sat on the charpoys (wooden frame traditionally strung with natural fiber, mostly rope) and others on the floor.

A big woman, taller than my grandfather by a foot, my grandmother had a strong voice. She ruled the house. I sensed everyone, including my grandfather, feared her, but not me. From her vantage point in the center of the courtyard, my grandmother gave orders.

"Jaggi, are the cows fed?"

"Devi, make sure the clothes are hung inside out to protect the colors."

"Sanju, you were late in milking the cows, and we have no time to churn fresh butter."

"Guddi, is there enough firewood for the stove?"

"Harbans Singh, did you lock the storeroom?"

And, on and on and on...

She carried a big bunch of keys with her all the time. The sound of these keys alerted us to her presence. I was most interested in one key. The key to the pantry where homemade biscuits, jams, sweat chutneys, and coconut macaroons were stored.

The house was always alive with women and men and often their children. Some were there to cook, some to wash clothes, some to bring in the wood, some to take care of the animals, some to sweep and some just to sit around my grandmother, sharing village gossip. I was happy having so many people around.

Years later I asked my mother if all these people worked for my grandfather. She said some did, and some just did errands on a barter system. Those were the old times, she said.

The Last Train

The summer of 1947 started like all other summers. In May, we, my mother, my baby sister, and I, packed our bags in Faridkot, where my father worked in the Department of Agriculture. We were going to Wadhai Cheema, the village home. As we had in the past, we took the train to Rayia, a one-room brick railway station serving the neighboring villages. I looked forward to my train ride on the noisy old coal-burning train with wooden shutters on the windows.

Even before the train started, I felt the soot as I knew I would sit with my head out of the window in the fast-moving air. I looked forward to the stops at the larger city train stations where vendors with baskets on their heads walked up and down the platform selling sweets, tea, biscuits and toffee. Once on the train, I eagerly waited for my mom to order the breakfast, which would be waiting for us at the next station.

From Rayia, we went to my grandfather's house. On this trip, luckily for me, my grandfather had sent a tonga. I was spared from riding the horses, unlike previous trips. When we reached the house, I rushed to my room with the stained-glass windows that shed wonderful colors across it. I lay on the bed and watched the colors flicker around and listened to the voices outside. I felt I belonged.

At the start of the summer, everything seemed normal. I would hear the village men who had come to talk with my grandfather. They talked about land issues, the price of grain, cattle, and the weather. They would all sit under the massive mango tree outside the house, and tea would be served throughout the day as my grandfather spoke with them. My grandmother, like other summers, held her court with the villagers who wanted to see her in the courtyard. I was always happy being in that house.

Then, towards the end of that summer of 1947, the atmosphere in the house began to change. More people came to see my grandparents, their voices hushed and nervous. Everyone moved more quietly and said little, doing the chores a bit faster, not sitting around to talk. I overheard bits and pieces of the adults' conversations. Often there was fear in their voices. I heard one woman telling my grandmother that everyone had been killed in another village. I did not understand who was killing who and why. But fear of death found a grounding in me.

Then one day, my mom announced that we were leaving. My dad had sent a message that it was not safe for us to stay in the village any longer. I wanted to stay longer. My grandparents were not leaving, so why were we? I asked my mother, but she remained silent.

By the time we got to the train station, there was utter confusion and chaos. There were people everywhere trying to leave on the train. My grandfather was crying, my mother was fussing over us, people were shoving their children through any open train window they could find. Two large men with turbans, long beards, large swords tied to their waists, met us at the station and led us into a compartment and stood at the door trying to keep people out, an impossible task.

My baby sister started crying, but I held my tears back. I was hungry but was afraid to ask for food. I was scared. I did not understand what was happening. Mothers' crying, fathers' crying, begging people to take their children on the train when they saw that the train was full. I wanted quietness to calm my unsettled and confused mind. I wanted my sister to stop crying.

Finally, the train started to move. I nestled close to my mother for warmth and gazed out of the window. I saw the desperation and hopelessness on the faces of those left behind.

"What will happen to them," I asked my mother.

"They will be fine," she said in a soft assuring voice as she closed the wooden shutters to the windows. I wondered if that was true but was comforted to hear it from her. I put my head on my mother's lap and dreamt of the flying sunlight coming through the window of my room in the huge white house we had left behind. I asked if my grandparents would come later. My mother just patted me on the head. My sister, exhausted from crying, fell asleep, and the train moved further and further away from the village house that I loved but knew by then was a thing of the past.

By August, India was divided into two countries: India and Pakistan. Approximately fifteen million people were displaced from their homes, and about two million people were killed. Wadhai Cheema was in Pakistan when the border was drawn. Our train was one of the last to make it across the border before all borders were closed.

The Forbidden River

I was aware of death that year, and the fear of death liberated me in a way that I did not understand then. I was five years old in 1947. My family was safely back at our house in Faridkot, cutting short our summer visit to my paternal grandparents' village in Wadhai Cheema. Faridkot is an old historic city in Punjab, North India, located near the border drawn in 1947 to partition India.

Our house was built around a courtyard. The three bedrooms were on one side of the courtyard, the living room on the other, and the kitchen, storerooms, and bathrooms on the third. A tall, cemented wall surrounded the house with a two-panel wooden gate for entrance, which made up the fourth side of the courtyard. The house was close to a gravel road that led to the border. As the news of the partition spread and riots began on both sides of the border, our house became a refuge for relatives and friends fleeing from

Pakistan. Refugees coming from and going to Pakistan stopped at our house to rest or for food and water.

My parents opened the house to all. I often felt that my house was taken away from me, but I was also happy to have many cousins who were temporarily staying with us as their parents waited for their compensatory land or house to be allocated to them by the government. The house was surrounded by vast farmland for agricultural research. A stream, a branch of the larger river Sutlej, passed through the western part of the property.

The Courtyard

All the rooms of the house opened onto a cemented courtyard where much of the day-to-day activity took place. The three medium-sized bedrooms held the suitcases piled up in the corners of all the relatives who were staying with us. At night, everyone slept outside in the courtyard on charpoys. Every night there were fifteen to twenty charpoys laid out. A lightweight cotton quilt was placed on the matted charpoys. Two cotton sheets, one for the bottom and one for the top, lay on each bed. I do not remember having pillows. The heat was unbearable at night. The bedrooms had ceiling fans, but there was not enough room for all. My parents slept in one of the bedrooms under a ceiling fan at full speed, giving an illusionary sense of coolness.

The kitchen area was the place to be. Just outside the kitchen, there were three fire pits, recently built. They were not there when we left early in the summer to visit my grandparents in Wadhai Cheema. On one of the fire pits, a huge steel pot cooked lentils in large quantities all day long. On the second, lay a flat, round, black cast-iron chapatti maker. Fresh chapattis, smelling of warm dough and ghee, were being made all day long, ready to be eaten. On the third, a big round copper pot in which tea with milk and sugar, flavored with cinnamon and cardamom, was steaming hot all day long. It created an aroma of welcome and warmth. Volunteers from the family and those passing by would help. A few charpoys were arranged close to the cooking area for people to sit and eat. There was a bucket of water and a basin with a mug for people to wash their hands before and after eating. There was no set or fixed time for meals. I heard pieces of conversation. Many of those who stopped had not eaten for days and were not sure when next they would eat a meal.

I found myself always hanging around the kitchen area. I can still taste the hot chapatti, which I would carefully hold closely in both my hands with crushed onions in the center. I would always ask for red peppers to be put on top by whoever was managing the outdoor kitchen. I was tired of lentils. I loved those hot chapatis with ghee and crushed pepper. We did have eggs some days, but the eggs were not enough for everyone.

Stealing Eggs

There was a large hen house outside the wall of the compound. Some mornings my mom would send me and my baby sister out to the hen house to fetch eggs. I liked playing the big sister and feeling responsible. I would hold my sister's hand (she had just barely started to walk upright) and lead her outside to the hen house. I would reach to open the latch to the chicken wire fence. We would step into the area where about ten boxes were spread out. The food bins situated in one corner of the fenced areas were filled with corn and some green stuff. The rest of the space was open for the hens to walk around. My sister would usually shuffle over to one hen sitting protectively on the eggs and, reaching under, would grab a warm egg. Before I could take it from her and put it in the basket, she would crack it and suck the raw egg. When I tried to stop her, she would get another and then another. I would run back to the house to tell my mother. I was sure my sister was going to die eating all those raw eggs.

The Charpoy

My parents had their hands full during that summer. In addition to managing the household, the farm, all the relatives, and the refugees, my maternal grandmother came to stay with us. Her frail body lay on the charpoy in the courtyard that was specially prepared for her each morning, a cotton mattress covered with white sheets, a grey blanket, and a pillow on which she rested her head. Her small, fragile frame merged to become one with the bed. Her bed was in the large courtyard near the entrance to the house. I remember a large tree providing shade and comfort from the summer heat. My mother sat next to her all day long or so it seemed to me.

I remember wanting to hug her when I would see my mother sitting next to her, but I was afraid of not knowing why she never got up. No one explained to me why she was in bed all the time. Later, I learned that she had had a stroke. No one ever said it aloud, leaving me to wonder why she did not want to talk to me. At some point during the same summer, the bed was no longer there, and mother said Grandmother had gone home to Peshawar, where my grandfather worked in the internal revenue services. My grandmother did not give me a goodbye hug. Mom said that my grandmother spoiled me, as I was her first grandchild. I wanted to remember what being spoiled felt like.

The Banyan Tree

There was a large Banyan tree on the property near the gravel road that led to the border. The shade from the vast branches, thick with leaves, provided solace from the heat. With nothing else to do but wait for news, the relatives and others living in the house would sit on charpoys all day long, watching the stream of refugees walking to or from the border.

Despite being told not to run around barefoot, which I found more comfortable in the heat than wearing shoes, I stepped on a bee one day. My foot swelled up to the size of a lemon, or it felt like it. I could not walk or play with the kids. My uncle would carry me each morning and place me under the banyan tree with the other relatives who had no other work to do but wait. I would sit under the tree, viewing the constant line of people silhouetted against the vast farmland with bundles on their heads, slowly moving step by step to and from the border. Some people were close enough for conversations.

"Is everyone safe in your family?"

"Who is still behind?"

"What are the conditions like on the other side?"

"Is all your family out?"

Some would break away from the line for water or for a quick meal at our house, where the lentils, chapattis and tea were fresh all day long.

After a while, I would lie down under a tree, with my swollen foot raised on a pillow, and gaze at the vast branches and rich green leaves that spread across the horizon. I would close my eyes and dream of the time when life would be normal again. I often thought of my Wadhai Cheema grandparents. One day when my dad was sitting under the Banyan tree to rest a while, I asked him about them. He just shook his head from side to side. I never understood what that nod meant. Were they alive or not, I wondered? But I was afraid to ask more.

Becoming Roosters

On any given day, there were six to eight kids ranging from the ages of two to sixteen around the house. We were unsupervised, and the older kids ruled the day. One day, the oldest teenager, who was my mother's youngest brother, talked us into taking a ride in the bullock cart to see what was happening beyond the forbidden boundaries of the farm.

The sun was setting, and a dusty pinkish sky awaited us by the time we returned. As we neared, I saw my mom with her hands on her waist, her feet strongly planted on the ground, waiting for us. I knew, as did the others, that we were in trouble. My mother said nothing, which was a bad sign. When we quietly piled, one by one, off the bullock cart, she commanded, "MurgaBano" (in English, "become a Rooster"), which meant we must get in line, bend our knees, spread our legs apart, put our arms behind and through the legs and reach for our ears and hold our earlobes.

Mom carried my sister, who was two years old, in her arms and walked into the gate to the courtyard of the house. "Do not move," she told us, turning back. Mom finally sent one of my aunts to release us from our rooster positions. I was not sure how long we stayed in that position, but I do remember my arms hurting and feeling envious that my sister got away easily.

Another day, one of the older cousins convinced us that it was time for us to learn how to smoke. We had no clue how to get the cigarettes, so we rolled up old newspapers into small cigarettes. One of the cousins sneaked into the kitchen and found a box of matches. We went to one of the vacant bedrooms, hid under a bed and lit our homemade cigarettes. The smoke, the choking and coughing, quickly brought my mother to the scene. The older kids were nowhere to be seen, so there I was with my two cousins, aged six and seven, dying, I thought, under the bed. All three of us became roosters again. I often wondered why mom did not think of another punishment, as being a rooster was not working to keep us out of trouble.

The Forbidden River

Despite being told many times by the elders to avoid the river, we kids found ourselves walking toward it one day. My sister, who was walking a little steadier by then, was with us. When we got to the bank, we saw bodies, bloated, and floating down the river. Some naked, some with no heads, some fully clothed, and some still little babies. At first, I did not know what I was seeing. Once I realized the truth, I grabbed my sister's hand.

I put my hand on her eyes and dragged her away from the scene, frightened at the knowledge of what I had seen. We all ran from the river. We never went back to the river for the rest of the summer; at least, I did not. I told no one what we had seen. I do not remember discussing it among us. I was hoping that the memory would go away by not talking about it, but it never did.

By the end of the summer of 1947, the relatives staying with us began to leave for places allotted to them by the government as compensation. Our life in the Faridkot house began to return to some normalcy. However, I started dreaming about death and dying. A dream that recurred often enough would frighten me and stayed with me until I was well into my teens. In the dream, I would be chased by a group of large men with swords. It would terrify me, and I would wake up soaked in sweat, just in time before they caught me or killed me. Over time the dream became less scary, and I would just run away from the men or face them, waiting for the inevitable. I stopped waking up in terror once I accepted that I was going to die.

That death is integral to living was a realization that came to me during that summer and, in some ways, set me free from its threat.

Grandparents

A bit worn out, black and white photographs of my grandparents hang on the wall in my house along with other pictures of the family. My maternal grandparents are sitting side by side in a picture taken in 1946, framed in a quarter inch of black wood. It has a black background and is four by six inches in size. My grandparents seem to take up all the space in the small frame. In comparison, my paternal grandparents' photograph is a family portrait and is much larger. They sit side by side in the center, surrounded by their two children and their spouses. On the floor at their feet are their three grandchildren. A one-inch black wooden frame surrounds the ten-by-twelve-inch family picture. I liked having the pictures on my wall, but I often wondered what do I know about them and how did they affect me? In my imagination, I believed they loved me.

Biji

Of my grandparents, I remember my maternal grandmother the least. In the photograph, she wears a white chunni, which half covers her head and is slightly draped across her shoulders. She wears round glasses. A shade of light color lipstick covers her thin lips. She wears round gold earrings with a matching necklace—all dressed up for a formal portrait with my grandfather sitting next to her. I was four years old when the picture was taken.

My mother called her Biji. I do not remember calling her by any name. My mother told me she was kind and soft-spoken and that she loved me. I have a vague memory of visiting my maternal grandparents as a toddler when they lived in Peshawar. I was three years old. My grandmother would sit on a large verandah of their colonial-style house in the mornings, and I would play near her. According to my mother, my grandmother would give in to whatever I wanted. I could do nothing wrong, and she hated to see me cry. I have a vague image of a fruit vender with his cart loaded with different fruits coming to the house. I would always want a watermelon—it must have been summer. My grandmother would spread a huge towel on the floor of the verandah, on top of which she would position me. She would cut the watermelon and put the large bowl with watermelon pieces in front of me, my mother tells me. I would eat as much as I wanted. My mother still talks about how the speed with which I ate and simultaneously peed was the same and a source of much amusement for all around. I still love watermelons.

Looking at the picture I try to feel Biji's love and gentleness based on my mother's description of her. At times I feel the warm sensation inside me—maybe she did hug me during those visits and when she was not sick. Her being kind stuck with me and when someone describes me as kind, I think of her.

The other memory of Biji from the summer of 1947 in the Faridkot house was of her lying on the charpoy, never getting up, with my mom sitting next to her. I did not know that she was sick. That memory constantly reminds me of the loss of not knowing her and a desire to be close to her before she left to die back in her house. She was forty-seven years old.

Beiji

I called my paternal grandmother Beiji because my father called her that. In the photograph on the wall, she wears no glasses.

She did otherwise. She wears a heavy-looking white shawl around her shoulders under which a lighter-weight chunni covers her head. It must have been winter when the picture was taken. She is simply dressed without jewelry or lipstick. She sits straight up, looking directly at the camera. Her square face is unsmiling. She sits beside my grandfather and appears taller than him. When I look at the picture, her expression reminds me of how she would look at me when I was young and would not listen to her. She would give me that stern gaze that would make me run to my mother every time. I remember Beiji as a strong woman—not someone I would go crying to, but someone who got things done. She was over six feet tall and towered over everyone, including my grandfather.

My first memory of Beiji was during one of our visits to Wadhai Cheema when I was four or five years old. At dawn, when the cows were milked, I could hear her ordering the staff who helped maintain the large house in the village. From her vantage point in the middle of the courtyard, sitting on a charpoy, she could see all the corners of the house. I waited for her to start the day. She held keys to the storeroom where my favorite homemade biscuits were stored in a large stainless container, and jars of jams and round yellow ladoos (Indian sweet) made of milk, sugar, ground nuts and cinnamon were locked up to be rationed out at her discretion. I always got my fair share of biscuits and sweets, despite my mother's objections. I assume that Beiji liked me. I feel that I am a little like her. I like managing, and I do get things done.

In 1947, Beiji and my grandfather had to flee Wadhai Cheema, the village where my grandfather's ancestors had lived for generations, to stay with us in Faridkot until they were allocated compensatory land by the Indian Government in Ranjit Bagh. It took until 1951 for them to get settled in Ranjit Bagh. During my first visit to their new house, I noticed that Beiji had softened a bit and did not seem as tall as I remembered her in the large village house in Wadhai Cheema. Her voice was more subdued when she gave orders to the help who came to cook and clean. I wondered if having lost their house, title, and money, she was now less confident and sure of life in general. But she still held the keys, although a smaller bunch, to all the rooms in the newly constructed house in Ranjit Bagh. The pantry, much smaller than the village house, was still the storage room for Punjabi homemade sweets, although not in the old quantities.

She still assigned chores, which now included me as I was older. One chore I liked was making my bed on the rooftop of the single-story house where some of us children slept at night. It was much cooler than indoors as we had no electricity for fans. Before it got dark, one of the helpers from the village would place a wooden ladder from the courtyard to the top of the roof and carry up five or six charpoys. Then, he would spread a thin cotton mattress on top. I liked taking the rest of my bedding, which included a sheet, a thin blanket, and a pillow, up myself when we were ready to sleep. I often made more than one trip. I, along with my sister or cousins, if they were visiting, would sit on our beds talking. I do not remember what we talked about, but I remember much laughter and giggling. I remember the quietness and the stars. When my grandfather climbed up the stairs, we knew it was time to be quiet. I would lie on my bed looking up at the dark sky lit up with the stars. Whispering to each other, we would play a game of "who can find the small and the big dipper first." With no electricity or vehicular traffic, the sky was so close and glittered with the bright stars that I wanted to reach out and touch them, wishing I could live among them.

Now, whenever I am in a place where the sky is clear, I look for the big and small dippers, and I can still hear Beiji instructing me and all the others about what needed to be done before we slept.

I was in college when Beiji died. My mother went to Ranjit Bagh. She told us that Beiji was sick, but no one told me how sick she was. A few days later, my sister and I were summoned. It was only when we got to the house and saw Beiji laid out on a bed with a white sheet covering her that we were told she had passed away. We were asked to give her a goodbye kiss, but I did not want to kiss her. No one told me that she had been sick with cancer. I did not cry, but I felt cheated that I could not say good-bye. I was hurt and angry at everyone for depriving me of that privilege.

Pitaji

I addressed my maternal grandfather as Pitaji because my mother did. I had the most complicated relationship with him. I respected him, but I was not sure that I loved him. In the picture, sitting next to Biji, he looks extremely official. He is wearing the traditional Sikh turban neatly around the head, a greyish suit, and a bright tie with paisley motifs. His beard, neatly trimmed and tucked, has more white hair than black. I can see a fancy chain hanging in his pocket by a pin on the coat lapel. I was told that at the other end was a pocket watch, a style of influential people in those days. It was a portrait taken during his work years under the British Raj. I have seen the same picture in my mother's family albums. I feel no emotion when I look at the picture.

I was seven years old when my parents sent me to Delhi to live with Pitaji. In 1949, my father was posted in Nabha which then did not have a good school. I was told that Delhi had good schools. I lived with him until I was fourteen. Pitaji enrolled me in the Presentation Convent school. He bought me my first musical instrument, the Sitar. He was the one who encouraged me to read. He was the one who ensured I participated in school sports. He was the one I would get angry at when he applied parental rules. I was never sure how to be with him. He was my grandfather trying to be my father, and that was confusing to me.

Some nights, I would go to his room to lie down with him, but his body lacked the warmth I needed from a parent, so I would get up and sadly go back to my bed. Looking back, I think he did the best he could. He must have been grieving for his wife, who had died just two years earlier. I am not sure he knew how to bring up and take care of a child. His own children were brought up by his wife, and when my grandmother got sick, he pulled my mother, the oldest of his kids, out of school to take care of the siblings. I never forgave him for not letting my mother complete high school. She wanted to be a doctor and wished she had finished school.

After he retired, he bought some land in the agricultural state of Punjab and called it "Hari Farm." Hari is the Punjabi word for green. Us kids, six of his grandchildren, loved the farm. It was a different experience for me as compared to being at Wadhai Cheema village. At the farm, we had all the land to ourselves to run around and play. We had a small, concrete swimming pool which was an extension of the farm water system, but big enough for us to swim and splash in. Pitaji let us roam around freely. I was the oldest of the kids and ruled their days, which secretly loved.

Over the years, Pitaji changed into an angry and mean person who, at times, I did not recognize or want to be around. At Hari Farm, he had an accident and lost his right arm at the elbow. He was showing a farmhand how to feed cane into the cane thresher. After the accident, he was never the same. His farm failed. He had to sell the farm at a loss and was taking turns living with his children. He was a diabetic and on insulin. By the time he was seventy, he was showing symptoms of dementia. Not much was known about Alzheimer's in India then. He finally moved into my parent's house as they had an extra bedroom. As his disease progressed, his behavior toward my mother grew more aggressive. I did not like that and resented him. I was afraid that he would hurt my mother, and I worried about that. He was always trying to get out of the house. He would tell my mother that he did not want to live with her.

Then one day, he did leave the house, and no one knew where he went or what happened to him. Despite extensive efforts through the media and the police, he was not found. I was in Ann Arbor finishing my PhD when Pitaji disappeared. I was horrified, especially for my mother's sake. I had mixed feelings about him. For a full year, I did not know how to grieve for him as we did not know if he was alive or dead. There was always hope that he would be found. My emotions about his death were mixed. I was glad that he was not around to be mean to my mother. I was also mad that he went missing since my mother might have felt guilty for not having taken better care of him. Although, she never mentioned it. But I was very sorry about how his life ended. After a year of waiting and hoping, my mother and her siblings decided to hold the end-of-life religious ceremony to give everyone some closure. I did not go to India for the ceremony.

I am not sure if I feel love for Pitaji as a grandfather, but I do owe him for ensuring that I had a well-rounded education. I did well in school. If I was lagging in a subject, he arranged special instructions after school. He helped me learn to value extracurricular activities such as music and sports. Music, sports, and reading have been an integral part of my adult life since then. I am forever thankful to him.

Paiaji

I liked my paternal grandfather the most. I did not spend much time with him except for summer holidays. I called him Paiaji as my father did. In his picture, sitting next to Beiji, he is dressed in the traditional men's

Pajama and Kurta, which men in rural North India wear. He has a white turban loosely worn over his head. His Kurta is white with no jacket. His beard is a bit unkempt and not as trimmed as Pitaji's. It is tucked back. His hands are folded in front of him. Sitting next to my tall grandmother, he appears so much shorter than he was. Although he was a person of authority as the head of a village when this picture was taken, his appearance and the way he is dressed are much more modest as compared to Pitaji. I remembered him as a quiet person, minding his business and never talking much.

As a toddler, I remember him in the Wadhai Cheema house as the village head. He would sit every day on the charpoy outside the house under a banyan tree. Many villagers, mostly men, would sit surrounding him on other charpoys. They would discuss village matters. He would let me sit with him sometimes, which I liked. It made me feel important and confident knowing that he let me be part of the grown-up world. I resented it when he sent me back to the house. I did not comprehend then why certain topics were out of bounds for toddlers. I wanted to know everything.

In 1947, he and my grandmother had to flee the violence. India was being partitioned, mainly on religious grounds, into two countries. Wadhai Cheema was part of the new Muslim country of Pakistan. They first lived with my parents in Faridkot and then were relocated to Ranjit Bagh where the Indian government allocated them land and a place to build a house as compensation. It was not until I was in school that they were settled and had built a house when we started visiting them in the summer holidays.

During those holidays, I remember Paiaji had a routine that he religiously maintained. Each morning after breakfast, he would get his cane and head out to the farm, which was mostly an orchard of mangoes and other fruit trees. Although it was leased to a farming family, he believed that daily supervision was important. I would walk with him most days. We would walk through the village as my grandparents' house was on the outskirts. He would stop and talk to the people, asking about their health, the status of their crops, and how their families were doing. I loved walking with him just as I liked sitting with him on a charpoy listening to the villagers talk about important matters back in Wadhai Cheema.

After my grandmother died, he maintained the house and the farm for a few years, and when his health started to affect his ability to keep up, he came to live with my parents. He still maintained his habit of walking each morning. He would walk at dawn. He would ask me to go with him. At times I protested when he would wake me up, sometimes at five in the morning, but once I got into a rhythm with his step and paid attention to the early morning quietness, and stillness, I started to enjoy my walks. We never spoke much. His walking habit became my habit over time. No matter where I am in the world, I still walk. Like him in Ranjit Bagh, as I walk, I find myself saying hello and greeting people along the way.

Paiaji was ninety-one years old when he died. I was living in the US then. My mother tells me that he returned from his morning walk and laid down on the charpoy in the verandah. He told her that he was not feeling so well and said, "I think it is time." Mom thought nothing of that statement and went to the kitchen to get him water, and when she returned with the glass of water in her hand, he had transcended. I did not go to India when he died. I felt sad at his loss, but I was glad that it was peaceful. I also thought it was a great way to leave this world, knowing that it was time. I want to leave this world like that.

I admired Paiaji and Beiji's resilience. They had lost everything during the India-Pakistan partition and moved across the border as refugees but rebuilt their lives from nothing. I never heard them complain about what they had lost. Some of that rubbed off on me. In times of difficulty, I think of them. In such times, thinking of them gives me courage.

Through writing about them, I have come to know my grandparents better. I see in my own actions and habits a little bit of each of them. I am struck by how much movement there was in my life from an early age. I was always visiting and going places. Historical events contributed to my grandparents' different moves to new houses and cities. My father's job took him to a new city every couple of years. For a child, all these moves must have made an impression. I see now that I chose a lifestyle and a career that made me move to new places every couple of years. I get a bit antsy after a few years in one place and want to move. But wherever I go, I bring with me photographs of my grandparents, parents and other family members and friends.

Reading in Chandigarh

In 1958, I had two years remaining to graduate from the Presentation Convent school, also known as St. Mary's all English Catholic school. Nine years earlier, I had come to Delhi to live with my grandfather. My father worked with the Indian Civil Service and then was posted in Nabha, a small city that did not have a reputable school. As a result, my parents decided to send me to live in Delhi, which at that time had the best schools in the country.

One late spring evening, my grandfather knocked on my bedroom door. He entered and sat down at the edge of my bed. I was comfortably reclined and reading, having finished my homework, and was getting ready to sleep. I was a little surprised as he seldom came to my room at that time of the night. He looked at me but did not meet my eyes. I was confused and asked if he was sick. He said that he wanted to talk to me about moving to Chandigarh, where my father was then posted, to live with my parents. He said that Chandigarh had a good high school. He had spoken to my parents, and the decision had been made. I was shocked and surprised. I was angry. Why had I not been consulted? I wondered as the meaning of his words sunk in. I loved my school. I would have to leave my best friends whom I had known since I was seven. I was on two sports teams. I was in the music chamber group. My grades were excellent. Had I done something wrong? I asked myself.

After my grandfather left the room, I wanted to talk to my mother, but calling at that time of the night was difficult. I tossed and turned and kept pondering what I might have done to cause my grandfather and my parents to make the decision to move me to Chandigarh.

I remembered one incident that might have upset my grandfather. A month or two earlier, a boy from my class came to the house to pick up a homework assignment that he had missed. We were sitting on my bed going over our homework when my grandfather entered the room. He was angry that I had brought a boy into my room without permission. I was fourteen years old, and I did not think I needed permission. My grandfather asked what we were doing and how long we had been there. His questions had an accusatory tone. My friend, scared by then, grabbed his books and left in a hurry. I was hugely embarrassed as I liked the boy and now was not sure if I would see him again. I was also mad at not being trusted. I slammed my bedroom door shut. I picked up a book randomly to distract my mind. My mother tells me that as a child, I had a habit of picking up a book and just turning the pages whenever I was upset, even before I knew how to read. I went on a hunger strike in protest at home but ate at school. When I did speak to my parents, they assured me that after so many years of living apart, they wanted me to move back home. But, I was not convinced.

My move to Chandigarh was not easy. I joined the new school just before the summer break. Chandigarh then was a small town compared to Delhi, the capital of India. My new classmates thought I was a city girl showing off about books, art, and music. They had no interest in being my friend. I thought they were ignorant small-town kids who read nothing and knew nothing. I did not need them. I missed my friends in Delhi and wallowed in my loneliness.

That first summer in Chandigarh, I turned to books for company. I came across the three-volume Holocaust Reader's Digest series on my mother's bookshelf. I read story after story hoping after hope for survival and a sign of humanity. After finishing the first book, I was stunned at how people in power created the laws to legalize their dreadful actions, laws which then provided justification and a defense for implementing their atrocities. Once done with the holocaust books, I turned to Tess of the d'Urbervilles by Thomas Hardy, hoping that the English countryside would provide some relief. I got lost in Tess's world of misery and misfortune in the social system and life in nineteenth-century England. I was also angry at her bad decisions and how men felt totally justified in taking advantage of her.

I read before going to school, after school and on weekends. My bedroom was my favorite place to read. I would prop up a couple of pillows to find the best position, and I read, oblivious to time and day. Often in the distance, I would hear my mom asking me to turn on the light and to not read in the dark or to eat something or that I should go out and play with my new friends. A horrible idea where I was concerned. It always surprised me that she worried about my reading when I remember her as always reading and her books neatly stacked in bookshelves.

I have always liked reading, but after moving to Chandigarh in the summer of 1958, reading took on a special meaning for me. It was not only an escape from loneliness, but I discovered pure joy in reading. I learned to get lost in the stories. I also started writing a journal that summer. Since then, reading and keeping a journal have become my lifelong passion. I have often asked myself if I would have loved reading and writing as much as I do if I had not made that move to Chandigarh. A move that was heartrendingly difficult that resulted in me finding a lifelong companion in reading and writing and never feeling lonely again.

The Photograph

A restored black and white photograph of her parents hangs in her condo hallway and has been in hallways in different houses where she has lived. The picture was taken on a trip during the summer of 1957. Gud's father had completed his PhD from Cornell University and was on a three-month tour of Europe, visiting agricultural universities and projects. Her mother joined him on the European tour.

Before Gud hung the photograph on the wall, she carried the smaller version in her wallet for many years. "1957 Paris France" was written in ink on the back of the photograph, which was worn out at the edges. Her parents sit at a round table in a restaurant with a bottle of champagne and a glass half-filled in front of each, looking at each other. Their chairs are half turned to face each other, close enough so they could touch. They seem completely engaged in conversation, unaware of people around them. Her mother is looking at her father questioningly and a bit mischievously. Her lips are parted, which could mean she is talking or smiling at something he said. The majestic presence of her father, she is sure, attracted some attention. He wears a turban, most likely maroon, a dark tie, probably blue, over the white shirt and black suit. His head is turned to face his wife, and he is attentively looking at her.

Gud's mother wears her favorite cashmere shawl embroidered with red roses. A gold necklace encircles her neck. Gud does not recognize the dress her mother is wearing. It is not the traditional Sari or the North Indian Salwar Kameez. Could it be a western dress? If so, she must have bought it in Paris and left it behind. In 1957 India, western dresses for women her mother's age were not acceptable attire.

Gud wondered why she had carried that picture in her wallet for so many years. Was it the look that her parents were sharing? Was it something missing in her parents' relationship as she was growing up which created the need for reassurance that, at one time, they were close? Had the way her parents looked at each other made her feel left out?

As Gud got older, the picture haunted her with questions about her parents. The look on their faces and drinking champagne in a restaurant in Paris is not how she thought of them. She remembers her mother as beautiful, a little aloof but practical, always present, always doing her work, always home. Her mother did not like social life and preferred reading. Gud thought of her father as a "bit stiff," a scotch drinker who never drank champagne. However, he was more socially active, and she knew he had a romantic heart when he told the story about how he fell in love with her mother.

"Our ancestors came from the same area in North India and had known each other for generations. We used to visit our villages as children, my family and your mom's family during the summer months. On one such trip, your mom and me happened to be with our parents on the same train in the same compartment. Your mom was seven years old, and I was eleven. As soon as I saw her, I thought to myself, one day, I am going to marry her. She was the most beautiful girl I had set my eyes on."

Gud never believed the story, which contradicted his official persona as a civil service officer in the government of India, but she loved listening to it and would ask him to repeat it at family gatherings. Her mother's version of the story was simpler and quite different. "We took that trip often, nearly every summer. Your dad was always there, but I did not think anything of it. I thought he was one of our cousins," she said dismissively. Every family in India has lots of cousins, even when you are not related. Long-term friends and even strangers are addressed by the young as auntie, uncle, or cousin. When Gud probed her mother more about her parent's relationship, the usual response would be something like, "What feelings? In my time, we did not sit around and analyze everything like you all do now or talk much about feelings and emotions. I took care of you kids, ran the household and he worked. We each knew what we had to do for you all and the rest of the family and our parents, and that is it."

The photograph had created an image in Gud's mind of a romance between her parents that she was not ready to let go of. She searched for other pictures from the trip and found one in front of the Trevi Fountain in Rome, then another in front of the Sphinx in Cairo. In each, they look happy, but at the end of their trip, the Moulin Rouge picture had that special look of togetherness. The trip must have reshaped their relationship in some way, Gud was convinced. According to Gud's mother, it was a trip of a lifetime. "It was the only trip your father and I had together. We saw Europe, people were nice to us and interested in our clothes and our thoughts. It is not important what I felt and thought then. It was memorable. Everyone thought your father was a prince, with his turban and all. I went with him wherever the program took us. I was happy to see so many new places."

After some time, Gud stopped asking her mother about the look in the photograph. She continued to enjoy looking at the picture, which is in a place where she can see it every time she leaves or enters the apartment. She often pauses and can feel the closeness in the look that her parents are sharing. The intimacy of their look continues to intrigue her in a nice warm way.

During Gud's recent visit to India, sitting with her mother late at night, the normal time when she and her mom have their quiet moments, her mother started talking about what it was like to be married.

"Your father was a good man, never got angry at me, but he had a bad habit of forgetting about me."

Hearing this shocked Gud. How could anyone ever forget her mother, who was so beautiful, royal and had a large presence in the house.

"He would call from the office and say, be ready at such and such time, we have an invitation to an event or a party. I would get dressed and wait and wait, and he would not come until late. I would learn then that he went straight from work. His excuse being that it was late, and he thought he would just go himself." Her mother paused and then said, "He forgot me often. Maybe he did not want me with him." Her voice sounded far away and full of remorse.

The image of her mother all dressed up, in anticipation of an evening out, waiting for hours for her husband to come home to pick her up, hurt Gud to the core. All her life Gud had believed that her mother was the one who did not like going out and often would feel sorry for her father having to go alone. Growing up, she would often encourage her mother to go out with her father and reprimand her often for letting him go alone. How little she knew.

Returning from the trip, Gud walked into her condo and, by habit, looked at the picture on the wall. The picture that seemed so perfect all these years now looked different, less romantic. Gud felt sad and wondered if she should take it off the wall or replace it with another.

Time on Her Hands

One cold December evening in Madison, Wisconsin, I entered my walk-in closet to get dressed. The six-by-eight-foot closet has a small chest of drawers facing me with my jewelry boxes and other knick-knacks positioned on top. The chest is covered by an ikat fabric from Uzbekistan. On the right are shelves. On one shelf, I had placed my multi-colored woolen skirts. I picked up a black and white skirt. I felt its warmth and a memory flashed in my mind.

My mother sits under a mango tree that spreads out lush and green, with unripe mangoes dangling; she's maybe knitting a sweater. A basket filled with green and blue yarn is at her feet, and her two cats lazily lounge on the second chair next to her. The year is 1976. My father is the Vice Chancellor of the Punjab Agriculture University in Ludhiana, India. My parents lived in a large house suitable for hosting university events.

The garden has mango, peach, and other fruit trees in the far-right corner. Red and yellow roses lined the other three sides with seasonal flowers mixed in.

My mother began knitting as a teenager when she had time on her hands during her school vacations. She taught herself to make sweaters, blankets, socks, and caps. Then she started knitting sweaters for everyone in the family. She knitted all the time. She even knitted in movie theaters. I have many pictures of my mother knitting. In one, she is sitting on a chair in front of a balcony that opened on the La Rambla when we were on a vacation in Barcelona. In another, she is in my living room in Yerevan, facing the balcony from which she could see Mt. Ararat when she visited me. I was posted there with US-AID. When she traveled on holidays to visit family and friends, her knitting paraphernalia traveled with her. Her knitting habit was an admirable conversational topic during our family get-togethers.

"Knitting is good for my aging hands," she would say as she grew older. "It keeps my mind occupied, and I don't have to think of stuff." She was referring to the grief she felt first for her father's death, then her husband's, my father, then her only grandson, and then my brother, her only son. To this statement, I had no response. The rhythmic movements of her hands and fingers soothed us as we sat together, with little to say, during the long, quiet, and dark evenings of grief after each death.

In the winter of 2014, my mother visited me in Madison, where I had retired. During the blistering cold winter, she wanted a project.

"Please make me a woolen skirt that I can wear over my tights to keep me warm," I asked her one day.

"What color would you like?" She sounded excited. Her knitting had found a renewed purpose.

I drove to a store and bought an indigo blue two-shaded yarn. Two weeks later, she handed me the skirt. I received many compliments from friends and strangers. When I mentioned to my mother that her skirt was much appreciated, she immediately wanted to make another.

"I have time on my hands. It will give me something to do during the winter," she said.

I bought yarn for two more skirts, a deep red one and a black and white one. She used an African motif design for the black and white skirt, which perfectly blended in with my mostly black and white wardrobe. The red skirt created a much-needed contrast to all the black and white.

When she was back in India, she continued to knit my skirts. Every time another family member visited India from the States, they had to carry back a skirt or two for me. As recently as 2021, when I visited India in January, she knitted me a deep blue and a red skirt. She said my other ones were getting old and that I should give them away, which is hard for me to do. Now I have twenty-two. I know that I do not need any more skirts, but the pleasure I hear in her voice when I tell her about the many compliments that I receive stops me from telling her—that I have enough.

My mom is ninety-eight years old as I write this. She continues to knit more skirts, and I continue to add them to the shelves of my walk-in closet. I know that a time will come when I hold these skirts close to my face, wanting to feel her smell and touch.

I have admired my mother since childhood. I thought she was the most beautiful person on earth. Later, as I learned more about her, this admiration turned into respect and awe. She never got to finish school because she had to take care of her siblings. Sending me to school at the age of seven to live away from her so that I could have a good education was her decision, even if it must have been emotionally difficult. Her belief that women are equal and can achieve whatever they aspire to, unique in her times, has made me who I am. Friends and family admire her resilience. Despite personal grief endured by all the deaths of those close to her, she has been the stable force in the family. She has a few mantras which have helped me during my life: mainly stay focused on the task at hand, stay mentally busy, take charge of responsibilities, don't indulge in self-pity, focus on the wellbeing of others, and never give up hope. I often wonder what choices she would have made if she had been able to finish her education and not get married at the age of fourteen.

Singing 99 Bottles of Coke on the Wall

In August 1975, I arrived in Ann Arbor, Michigan, and was assigned to a two-bedroom apartment in a housing complex managed by the International Ecumenical Center. Four students shared the apartment. A student from Puerto Rico and another from Japan occupied the larger of the two bedrooms. I moved into the smaller room and waited for my roommate. I had no information about her.

My new roommate was a woman named Sandra, who was studying to become a psychologist. I was working on my PhD to become a development advisor and work overseas. Two single beds could not fit in our small room, so we took the frame off one bed and put the mattress on the floor. I took that mattress as I like hard beds. There was no room left for dressers. We put Sandra's dresser in the closet. We moved mine to the living room. We got rid of all the clothes that did not fit within the shared wardrobe and the dressers.

Sandra had moved from Philadelphia for her post-graduate work. I had moved from India after an unpleasant divorce to continue my studies, which had been interrupted by that unnecessary marriage. Sandra is black, of African heritage, and I am muddy brown of Indian heritage. Sandra had a low-paying part-time job for a couple of hours a week. I had four hundred dollars per month in alimony from my ex-husband. I should have settled for more. Our tuition was covered by scholarships, but even with the best of budgeting, we were always short of money after paying rent, utilities, and basic food bills. We both felt a bit out of place in Ann Arbor. Sandra had grown up in Philadelphia, and I had moved from India to make the United States my new home.

Sandra had a beautiful face and a singer's voice. She spoke English with a Philadelphia accent. She went to great lengths to straighten her very thick and curly hair, even in those days when Afros were in style. She dated black men and white men, but she did not hang out with either.

"I don't fit in with my 'peeps,' she would lament. "Why do I have to be anything but myself? I am not black enough, and my accent is too white, I am told by my black acquaintances. And the white folks think I'm trying to be white."

I was a good sounding board, as I understood very little then about the American issues of race and culture. Listening to her, I became intimately aware of the struggles and difficulties of being black in America and trying to lead a normal life. Each day, there would be some incident that reminded her of her blackness, and this was in Ann Arbor, a liberal university town. What must it be like for someone like her elsewhere in the country? I wondered.

Sandra had a nightly ritual to straighten her hair that fascinated me. She would sit at the edge of her bed with twelve huge pink plastic curlers. She would take a handful of hair and wind her hair around one. Then she would affix two long steel pins to hold her hair to the curler. An hour later, the twelve curlers were a huge nest over which she would tie a scarf. I would watch this process every night lying on the mattress, wondering how she could sleep with those curlers.

I would tell her that she could save a lot of time if she just cut her hair shorter. Time that she needed. Sandra was always late, from getting to classes to finishing her papers or meeting a friend. Once her hair was curled and the scarf tightly knotted, the curls in place, she would kneel beside her bed and say her prayers. There was not much space between the edge of her bed and the edge of my mattress, so she often knelt on my mattress. She always said a prayer for me, even when I told her that I was fine. Her response was that a little prayer hurt no one. So, I gave up protesting. I would shut my eyes and listen to the prayers whispered in her melodic voice. Once done with her prayers, she would sit at one edge of my mattress, and we would talk.

In the morning, the curlers would come off, and she would comb her thick black hair straight downwards on both sides of her face, hiding it. It would frustrate me as I thought she had a beautiful face with smooth midnight skin. When I suggested that she let her face be seen, she would say, "hiding my face protects my soul." She also would never sing except in the shower. She claimed that she did not sing well enough when I encouraged her to sing more as I thought she had a lovely voice.

In 1979, the Ecumenical Center upgraded my status to a single-room apartment. By then, I had a part-time job and could afford it. Sandra moved to an off-campus apartment on the North Campus. For the next two years, we continued to meet and spend as much time together as our separate schedules allowed. On difficult days, we would meet at the common grounds and walk around the campus singing 99 bottles of Coke on the wall all the way to one bottle on the wall. We would giggle and laugh, but we always felt hopeful by the time there was one bottle on the wall. That was the only time that I heard Sandra sing outside of her shower.

We each finished our degrees in 1980. Sandra moved to Detroit and worked as a clinical psychologist on a ward in a general hospital for a couple of years before moving to the east coast. I moved to Washington, DC, to pursue my dreams in international development. I finally joined the foreign service and moved overseas. Over the next thirty years or so, until 2012, when I retired and moved back to the US, we kept in touch by long newsy letters as calling overseas was both expensive and not convenient. She visited me with her family when I was posted in Ghana and after my retirement when I moved to Madison. I made it a point to visit her during my years overseas when I would come to the US on leave.

I have often wondered about the basis of our friendship. What has kept us close for so many years when most of those years we were thousands of miles apart? Our coming together in the small space of that apartment in Ann Arbor, not knowing anyone else and needing support from each other, could be one reason. Another more important reason, I believe, was our lack of any cultural biases. I had not known much about the African American culture, and she had not been close to someone with Asian Indian heritage before she met me. Thus, we might have found a basis for our friendship in a completely open way, free from preconceived opinions. To this day, I never feel judged by her, and I never feel that I must explain myself to her. I hope she feels the same. So many years later, we still find ourselves singing 99 bottles of Coke on the wall and ending up laughing, just as we did in Ann Arbor.

Dupont Circle

In 1981, I moved to Washington, DC, from Ann Arbor. I had finished my postgraduate work and was hired by Battelle for my first job in international development. I felt elated at having found a job in my field of expertise and at the prospect of living in Washington, DC. I found a house on Q Street in Georgetown that I shared with a friend. I would spend my weekends taking long walks and exploring the city. Walking from Georgetown to downtown was an easy walk for me.

My preferred route was down Wisconsin Avenue, window shopping at the fancy stores. I would then turn left on M Street and wind my way to Dupont Circle. The Dupont Circle neighborhood, with its Bohemian atmosphere and its small cafes and eateries, appealed to me.

The Kramerbooks and Afterwards, the first bookstore/café in the US, which opened in 1976, was located there. It had the best selection of books. I would browse for hours and would forget about the time, and I often took the bus back to M street.

On sunny days, I would sit on a bench in Dupont Circle and just people-watch. The scene then consisted of older people, mostly men, playing chess and or sitting around and talking. Watching the older men, I would often think of my father. He had recently retired from the Indian Civil Service but continued to do consultancy work to stay professionally active. My parents lived in India, and he was planning to visit me in the summer. I was looking forward to showing him the city through my eyes. I felt that my career and life journey had found its trajectory, and I wanted to share my success with him. I also hoped to come closer to my father during this visit.

I did not know my father well. I do not remember spending much time with him growing up. I remember him going to work and coming home late. My mother would tell me to be quiet when he came home because he had a busy day. All his days seemed to be busy days. I do not remember him playing with me or hugging me. I do not remember him ever being angry or ever speaking harshly to me. I was aware of his presence all the time, even though he did not seem to be aware of mine. My mother told a story about how he forgot my first name when he took me to be registered at my first formal school at the age of six. But I loved him nevertheless, and I knew he loved me.

My father was born into a farming family. My grandfather Paiaji had high expectations of his only son. Paiaji did not want his son to be a farmer, so education became a high priority. The nearest school was five miles away, which my father walked to and back from each day. Paiaji told me that my father never had time to play. By the time he got back from school and finished his homework, it was time to sleep and then up again for the long walk to school. That could be one reason that my father never quite knew how to have fun and was always busy and aloof. There were times that I wanted to run up to him and put my arms around him to hug him. Maybe if I had done just that, he would have lifted me in the air and swung me around and hugged me, but I never had the courage.

This distance between us remained during my adult life. Although not close emotionally, I learned from listening to him and watching him, that hard work pays off, that treating everyone equally is key to humanity, that being comfortable in our own selves helps us overcome hurdles and difficulties. I was looking forward to his trip. I wanted him to know me being a bit like him as an adult. I wanted to share much with him hoping to make up for lost time.

In May 1982, I lost my job due to budget cuts. I moved in with a friend of my parents who had a house in the suburbs of Arlington. She had recently lost her husband and needed company, and I needed a room until I found another job. Unfortunately, she drank, and I was not in a good place to provide her company. I was devastated at the loss of my first job. But I was nonetheless excited and looking forward to my father's visit in July when his consultancy job in Africa was completed. His visit gave me hope at a difficult time in my life.

On the evening of July 17, which would have been the morning of July 18 in India, I was visiting friends I had known since 1971 and who were more like family to me. They also lived in Arlington, not far from where I had moved. We had just finished dinner, a healthy summer salad, and were still working on our wine. My friend went to the kitchen to clean up, and I thought I would complete a job application. My glass of wine was half full. Suddenly, I felt uneasy. A feeling of heaviness and sadness overtook me. I thought that I was getting sick. I had a strong feeling that something in my world order had shifted, like an earthquake. I had to leave. It was 9:00 p.m.

When I arrived at my friend's house, I quietly opened the front door and cautiously entered. I saw her lying drunk on the carpeted staircase halfway between the landing and her bedroom. She looked up and mumbled, "Amrik died." My father's first name did not register for a second. He was in his sixties and in good health. I thought I must have heard her wrong or that she had made a mistake. I slowly walked to the phone and called my sister in California. She had received a call about his death from one of our relatives in India. She did not have any more details except that he had finished his consultancy work and was at the Serengeti Resort in East Africa for the weekend before intending to return to New Delhi.

After I got off the phone, not knowing what else to do, I went and sat next to our drunk friend. I felt extremely tired. I could not get up from the stairs. I wanted to lie on the stairs and forget what I had heard. I just sat there. I felt no pain, just numbness. After some time had passed, I was not sure how much, I went to my bedroom and took out a suitcase from the closet. I looked at my clothes but could not figure out where to start. I lay down and went to sleep, fully clothed. Sometime later, I found myself sitting in bed sobbing. My friend, who had sobered up some, brought me a hot cup of tea.

I was able to leave the next day on a PANAM flight that departed from Dulles International. Once on board the plane, my body wanted to sleep, but questions raged in my mind. What had really happened? He had all his medical clearances, and no one had ever mentioned any health problems. How did he die? Did he suffer before dying? Why did he not call out for help? On and on, my mind raced. I felt that I had been unfairly orphaned too young. I was forty years old. Then I remembered that I still had my mother, but it felt different.

I would learn later that my father had woken up, showered, and dressed to return to Nairobi to catch his flight to New Delhi. When he did not show up for breakfast, a colleague went to his room and found him kneeling at the side of the bed. The death certificate said asthma-related heart attack. I stayed with my mother for a month. I made three trips to India during the next twelve months to help in whatever way I could. My father, not expecting to die, had left little paperwork behind, which would have helped my mother deal with the bureaucratic inheritance issues.

When I returned to the US, I was completely lost. I stopped looking for jobs. I no longer knew why I was in the US or what I wanted to do with my life. I did not get out of bed for days at a time. I could not make sense of my life and wondered if I should move back to India. I thought of my mother. Did she need me? I was afraid to lose her, also. Should I give up my career and move back?

When I asked her, my mother said, "Absolutely not. You must make your own life. What has happened has happened. I will be fine."

So going back to India was not an option and my mother, I knew, wanted me to make a life for myself that was fulfilling to me. She had always put a high priority on my being independent. I started looking for a place to live. I knew that my being around my friend's drinking was not healthy for me. At times, I admit, it was an attractive escape to my grief, but I resisted. I found an affordable efficiency apartment in Arlington near

Glebe Road. I started looking for a job again. I had only a few months remaining on my unemployment benefits. When those funds dried up and I still did not have a job, I sold some gold jewelry that I had from my wedding and was of no use to me, to pay rent. I was hopeful that I would find a job. I was too proud to ask my parents for help. For some time, I lived as two selves. One who would manage to somehow get dressed, go on job interviews, and do the essential activities to appear alive. My other self would appear when I entered my apartment, often collapsing on the bed, crying uncontrollably, without any sense of purpose, time, or life. The hollowness I felt inside was deep, and I felt I could not free myself of it.

Slowly, life started to take over. I did manage to get short-term jobs with the World Bank and the UN, which kept me afloat for a year or so. In 1985, I applied for a job with an international organization implementing a regional USAID operations research project in Asia, with its head office located in Bangladesh. I moved to Bangladesh. Contract work gave me the economic stability that I so needed and the experience in international work that I wanted. But it was not a lifelong career plan for me. I was looking for a more permanent job with more responsibility and benefits. I was in my forties and was thinking more and more about savings for retirement. When a position opened in USAID mission in Bangladesh, I applied and was accepted. The position was for a year, but it gave me the opportunity to know US-AID's values and policies. I liked working for USAID. I felt I could relate to its vision. When USAID opened some career positions for health officers in 1990, I applied and was relieved when I was accepted.

"I will be fine." My mother's words stuck with me. But I have never been completely fine. My father's death was like an unexpected knock on the door, an unwelcome guest, one that I was not ready for, and nor did I want in my house. There were so many unanswered questions I asked myself then and still ask myself now. Would it have been different if he had not been in Africa in a remote place? Would it have made a difference if he had immediate medical help? Why did he not share information about his asthma or heart condition with anyone in the family, and would that have made a difference? I am not sure if I will ever find the answers to these questions or come to terms with the shock of his death.

When I visited Washington, DC, in 2017, I found myself drawn to Dupont Circle. I sat on one of the benches and thought of my father and that visit that I wanted so badly to happen. That visit on which I had put so much hope and faith to start a new and closer relationship with my father. The loss that I felt of not having known my father or having spent time with him remained strong inside me. Sitting there in Dupont Circle on a metal bench facing the sun, I came to accept that loss has no end nor resolution, and the unwelcomed guest remains forever inside your house. I missed him all my life when he was alive, and I continue to miss him now, more so in his death, all these years later.

Landing in Ouagadougou

I had just settled in my Air France seat for the six-hour trip from Paris to Ouagadougou when the passenger next to me began a conversation. He apparently assumed that anyone going to Burkina Faso, a former French colony, must be fluent in French. I managed to say *"Je parle un peu francais."* This quietened him, but my heart was racing. What am I going to do, and how will I get around and do my job, if I cannot say more than 'I speak a little French?'

I was working in Bangladesh when I heard that I had been accepted in USAID. I moved to Washington, DC, for the required language training and orientation. Burkina Faso was my first assignment as a foreign service officer with USAID. When I joined US-AID in 1991, I had never heard of Ouagadougou. After a year of orientation, I was more knowledgeable about the country. I was excited to learn a new language and experience a new continent and culture. French was the official working language in Burkina Faso and a requirement for my job.

I struggled with French lessons for six months. I grew up learning several languages: English, Punjabi, Hindi, and some Urdu. I thought nothing of it and was looking forward to being at the language institute. I always thought French was a fashionable language and was glad to have the opportunity to learn it. I was horrified when I failed the first two exams. My mental block about learning French was a result of my teacher's attitude toward anyone who did not try to speak like a Parisian.

After one exam, the teacher told me that I had no aptitude for learning a language. I found that insulting. Maybe I could not speak like a Parisian, I thought, but I was going to work and live in West Africa, not Paris! I requested to change classes. My next teacher was a French speaker from West Africa and more accepting of non-Parisian French accents. I passed the required test and was finally on the plane to Ouagadougou.

We landed in Ouagadougou at 3:00 a.m. in darkness except for the runway landing lights. I looked out of the window, thinking there must be a city somewhere. There were dim lights scattered around. My host from the embassy met me at the bottom of the flight ramp, a diplomatic privilege in 1991. We went to a special gate for diplomats where the embassy vehicle was parked. The expediter took my passport to clear my luggage through customs and other formalities. I did not have to be present. This was all wonderfully new to me.

I was able to mutter "*Bonjour, comment-allez vous*," the formal good morning, how are you to the driver. "*Bien, Merci*," was all he said. I was relieved that he did not want to talk more. We drove out of the airport onto a road with no streetlights. Everything around was in darkness. I could barely make out the shapes of concrete houses and mud huts. I thought to myself: where is this place?

Finally, we were driving on a paved road lined with trees and streetlights. I was told by my host that we were passing through the diplomatic area of embassies, including the American embassy. We passed a large two-story white house that was the US ambassador's residence. We stopped two blocks further in front of a metal gate with bars. I saw a figure on the other side of the gate, huddled up on a chair, fast asleep. He was the night guard. The driver muttering something in French, got out of the car to wake him up so he could open the door for us to enter the premises of the guest house where I was going to live for two weeks.

My permanent house was not ready yet, I was told by my host. My host unlocked the door. She handed me the welcome package consisting of the embassy phone directory, whom to call in an emergency and other touristy information about the city. My mind was in a fog, and I hardly heard much. I was exhausted from the long flight. I needed sleep, and I needed water. She told me that the welcome kit was all there, some basics such as water, tea bags, sugar, milk, bread, and juices to get me by till I could go to the store. "Do not drink tap water" was her one instruction before she left.

I was thirsty to the point of being slightly lightheaded. I opened the refrigerator and reached in to get a bottle of clear yellow liquid that looked like orange or lime juice. I opened the top and took two large sips. Immediately, I choked. I knew I had absorbed liquid not meant to be in my body. I looked at the bottle and the label read Javel—bleach, according to my dictionary. Who puts bleach in a refrigerator? I thought. I spent the next two hours drinking water and sticking my fingers in my throat to throw up. I was too embarrassed to call the embassy. At 5:00 a.m., the expediter brought my luggage. I made a cup of tea and went out to the yard to get fresh air. I could not sleep.

I went to the main gate, where the night guard was fast asleep again. I heard hushed voices and looked out through the bars of the locked gate. From the shadows of the early morning light emerged two tall, lanky men with deep brown skin. They had large indigo headgear. Their faces were covered with part of the material from the headgear. I could see only their eyes, which were lined with kohl. Small leather sheaths with knives stuck out of their belts. They wore silver jewelry bracelets, armlets, and necklaces. They walked majestically like they owned the street. Each of the men held a leash leading five camels. I was breathless. I had never seen something like this. I felt like I was in the Peter O'Toole movie Lawrence of Arabia. I was rooted to the gate, straining my neck to watch the last of the camels disappear out of sight. I knew then that I was going to like Burkina Faso. I was told later that the people I had seen were from the Tuareg tribe and were experts at making leather and silver goods.

I returned to my room and got dressed for my first day of work. My host arrived at

8:00 a.m. to take me to the embassy. That first morning consisted of a walk through the embassy compound to show me the layout of the different offices. At the end of the walk, my host brought me to my office and introduced me to my secretary, Aminata, whose name meant faithful and trustworthy. She lived up to her name during my four years of work in Ouagadougou. Aminata was dressed in the traditional professional outfit—a long colorful dress made up of Bazin combed fabric with a matching blouse. Her headgear stood out the most—a purple wrap decoratively tied around the head like a hat. I liked Aminata instantly.

By 3:00 p.m., I walked back to my apartment and took a much-needed nap. I was fast asleep when the guard knocked on my door. I looked out of the window and saw that it was evening already. As part of my welcome, my host had arranged an evening event for me to meet the American community. Her driver had come to pick me up. When we turned off the main embassy road onto an unpaved dirt road, I saw large cement houses surrounded by a security wall. My driver said that we were in the French section of town where most of the Americans also lived. That explained the better houses.

The welcome event was in a large garden, lit up with strings of white lights against the black Sahara night. In the soft lights, I could see people scattered around with glasses in their hands. Others were seated at small round tables eating. On one side of the garden, I could see a buffet dinner on tables covered with white tablecloths. On the other side was the bar. Each location was attended by servers all dressed in white with black ties. At the far end, I could see a swimming pool. On a small stage near the bar, three Burkinabe musicians played drums and a guitar as background music. I was not sure which world I had entered. I was starving and started to head toward the food and drinks. But my host guided me first through the crowd to introduce me.

After the introductions and a short welcome speech by my host, I headed to the bar. I knew no one and needed something to get the energy to be social. I asked the bartender for a glass of white wine. As I held a glass of wine, I heard a group talking about baseball and other sports. I tentatively approached them. I shared my limited experience in baseball and football, but I said I like racket sports. Jeffrey, one of the guests, mentioned that there were tennis courts and a squash court at the international sports club. He said if I wanted to play, he would be happy to play with me and said how about tomorrow evening. I was a little taken aback but said fine. I had no plans. I was not sure if he was just making conversation or if he was serious. As I moved away, I wondered who he was. I liked that he had asked me to play squash with him.

The next morning when I went to work, I noticed that Jeffrey's office was across from mine. The sign on the door read Jeffrey Wright, Famine Early Warning System (FEWS) Project Director. I had been briefed on his project in my orientation, along with all other programs USAID was supporting in Burkina Faso. I was going to be head of the health office, primarily supervising HIV\AIDs and Maternal Child Health programs. My first full day of work included briefing meetings. First with my USAID director, then with the ambassador, followed by security and health briefings. I did not tell the nurse at the health unit that I drank bleach the night before. I did not want to cause concern.

By 5:00 p.m., I wanted to get back to my apartment and sleep. By the time I reached the guest house, two blocks away, Jeffrey was there to pick me up for our squash game.

He came on his motorcycle, a Tenere, which I learned later is a good desert bike. I was a little surprised at the motorcycle, but it made Jeffrey a little more interesting to me. Tired and jet lagged as I was, I thought a game of squash would do me good. Riding to the sports club at the back of Jeffrey's motorcycle with the Sahel dusty wind blowing on my face, I thought this could turn out to be an interesting post. Little did I know then that it was the start of a romance in the Sahel.

Leaving Burkina Faso

My work in Burkina Faso turned out to be heartbreaking, challenging, and a powerful learning experience. HIV/AIDS had reached pandemic levels, and we were fast losing our Burkinabe staff at the embassy. Despite widespread preventive messages, it was difficult to change a culture rooted in polygamy and accepting of having many partners outside of the marriage. Condoms were widely available through our assistance program but getting people to use them was another matter.

The Burkinabe coordinator managing our HIV/AIDs program, who was well-informed about prevention measures, was dying of the disease. On a visit sitting at his bedside in the Ouaga hospital wing for HIV\AIDS patients, I hurt seeing his sunken eyes in a body that resembled a ten-year-old. He told me about his third marriage to a younger woman, who was also diagnosed with AIDS along with his other wives. I looked at him, and he knew what I was thinking—Bruno, you knew better. He shrugged and said, such is our custom. I felt sad. It was my first lesson about the clash between deep-rooted cultural practices and new interventions.

Burkina Faso opened a new world for me that I had no idea existed. Until then, Africa, for me, had meant game parks and poverty. Burkina Faso was poor, but its large number of ethnic tribes with their own cultures and lifestyle made it a special place for me. A mask-dancing ceremony late in the darkness of the night brought a level of excitement and fear that I had not experienced before. Dancers, no one knew who, wore masks representing antelopes and other wild animals and would dance all night, imitating the movements of the animals to bring fertility to the land. People would join in the dancing resulting in a trance-like atmosphere that was unnerving to outsiders like me.

The Tuaregs, a Berber ethnic group, who lived on the outskirts of Ouagadougou, opened their home to me. I remembered seeing the men leading their camels on my first day. I learned that there was an enclave of houses in one of the city neighborhoods where the Tuaregs lived. I visited them first to buy leather boxes and silver jewelry. After that, I started to stop by and was always welcomed. The women did not speak French, and I used hand language to communicate. The kids who went to school did speak some French and would help translate. I would sit on the floor on a mat with them. I am not very fond of camel milk but ate the nuts they offered. I bought lots of silver jewelry and leather boxes during my stay in Ouagadougou. It was my entry into their world that I never really understood.

By the time I left Burkina, I was rather humbled. I realized that with all my degrees and expertise, there was so much more that I needed to learn if I was going to be good at my job. US development assistance was being cut in Burkina Faso, and I had to close our USAID office by the time I left. Looking back, it was the hardest policy decision I had to implement in my career. So many people, especially in the health sector, depended on our assistance.

Burkina Faso will always remain special to me. It brought Jeff into my life. It was my first assignment with USAID. My first tour as a diplomat representing the US in a foreign country. My first experience in being responsible and accountable for the well-being of those I supervised. My first experience at saying goodbye to so many who became like my family for nearly five years and who I might never see again. My first lessons in diplomacy as a US official when I negotiated assistance needs and programs with host counterparts and other donors. My first experience working closely with our ambassador and the country team, which is made up of all agency and office heads in each US mission for coordination purposes. My first realization that having a supportive ambassador, who had my back, along with willing and collaborative Burkina counterparts, was key to my own success at my job.

In 1995, I was assigned to USAID Central Asia Regional Mission. Jeff and I decided to get married three weeks before my departure in September. My household effects were packed and shipped. The house was bare. The wedding reception hosted by our ambassador and his wife at the official residence made up for the emptiness I felt in my heart at leaving Burkina Faso, where I had learned so much from the people and the place. The wedding reception with friends and colleagues, dancing to the Burkinabe drumming, was the best going-away party of my life. Jeffrey stayed behind in Africa for six months to complete his contract with the FEWS project.

Landing in Almaty

I had just flown from DC to Frankfurt on my way to Almaty, the capital of Kazakhstan at the time. It was September 1995. Compared to the newly introduced Boeing 777, which I had flown from DC, the plane to Almaty was the older version of Boeing 737. There were no television screens and the seats hardly reclined. Everything looked worn out. Apparently, Frankfurt-Almaty was not the prized route for airlines then. The Boeing 737 was parked at the furthest end of the Frankfurt airport. I knew extraordinarily little about Kazakhstan, where I was headed to live for the next two to three years. Kazakhstan had been part of the vast Soviet Union until its dissolution in 1991 and was known as the "Steppes" to the outside world.

Most of my fellow passengers spoke Russian. When drinks were served after we reached cruising altitude, they all ordered vodka. When lunch was served, I ordered a glass of wine. My fellow Russian speakers continued with their vodkas. How much vodka can one consume? I wondered. Little did I know then that vodka was the drink of choice in Kazakhstan for breakfast, lunch and dinner, and any other time. I already felt out of place with my glass of wine.

We landed in Almaty around 10:00 p.m. in pitch dark, and the pilot waited for a long time to be told where to park the plane. Once in its allocated place, the pilot turned off the engines, but nothing happened. We all just sat and waited. Looking out of the window, I saw men in long army coats all around the plane on the dark tarmac. Three men stood at the bottom of the steps. I saw two airline staff members negotiating with them or showing them some papers. No one seemed to understand each other.

Finally, we were allowed to disembark. There was an archaic blue and white bus parked close by, but no one could tell us what we should do next—should we be allowed to walk, or should we board the bus? We all stood silently in line, not sure what to do. Finally, someone shouted out a word I did not understand and made a gesture for us to get on the bus. After fifteen minutes of driving in the dark, the bus stopped in front of a metal door. We got off the bus, but the door was locked, and people just looked around. We discovered that all passengers had to disembark from the bus before the security guard opened only one side of the door to let us into a small arrival room. Opening only one side of the entry and exit doors at official buildings then was a rule that I never understood.

I was met by my American boss. The arrival lounge was small and stuffy without windows. She had a bunch of red roses in her hands, which was a welcoming sight. The embassy expediter was with her to help me through the passport control and custom clearances. She took my passport and disappeared. A while later, she returned with a stern-looking official in an army uniform who was holding my passport in his hand. He approached me. He looked at my passport picture again and then back at me. He turned the passport to check the front cover to confirm my diplomatic status. He did this a couple of times, and I did not know what to do or say. I just stared back and waited. It was all new to me, as I am sure it was for him, as we were one of the first groups of Americans to be in Kazakhstan as diplomats. Finally, he moved us through many control checkpoints holding my passport in his hand with his arm extended above others shouting, "diplomat, diplomat." I was a bit embarrassed as people around turned to look at me and by the special attention I was getting.

It took an hour for my luggage to arrive in an even smaller room on a worn-out conveyor belt which crunched along at a snail's speed. Once my bags were retrieved, we exited to face a wall of men offering taxi service in their private cars, as there were no official taxi services, I was told. We pushed through bodies, with the expeditor repeatedly saying in Russian that we had our transport.

The embassy driver loaded my five bags into a black Chevrolet Suburban. I was told to bring everything I would need for a couple of months in case the rest of my household effects got delayed. We drove off on a massive boulevard with no streetlights. People in black jackets and coats, who could hardly be seen in the dark, crossed the road at all places between fast-moving cars. I wanted to ask if many got hit by the cars but resisted. I did not want to embarrass my Kazakh colleagues. Twenty minutes later, we entered a dark lane lined with trees and stopped in front of an apartment building that seem to stretch across the whole block. The steel door at the entrance had no overhead light The driver, using the light from a cigarette lighter was able to open the door.

We climbed the four stories to my new apartment, dragging my luggage. The staircase was pitch dark. The entry hall in front of my apartment had a small light bulb which was installed by the embassy as a security measure. On entering the apartment, I was struck by its opulent décor. Embroidered curtains, chandeliers as overhead lights, and bold color flowers and bird-printed wallpaper in each room. I was told that it was typical of the decor and options then available in Kazakhstan.

It was after midnight when my boss left with the warning, "Do not open the door to anyone. If they bang, let them bang and they will go away after some time. I will call you tomorrow." Wide awake, I wandered around the apartment. My inner clock was on Washington, DC time.

The next morning, I looked out of an my glassed-in balcony facing the main boulevard. I saw two- and three-story plain brick and steel buildings that stretched across a whole block. Through a narrow opening between the two buildings, I could see a glimpse of the Altai mountain range in the distance. Across the street were three small square wooden structures which looked like temporary roadside stands serving as shops, referred to as kiosks, I learned later. I saw fresh bread being delivered at the first one, and I was suddenly hungry. With a dictionary in hand and some local currency, Tenge, that my boss had given me, I left the apartment. I tentatively approached the first shop. A young Kazakh man looked questioningly at me through a small glass window that was half open. I said *"khleb,"* bread in Russian. He responded with a long questioning sentence. Not understanding him, I pointed to the round bread buns closest to me in the window case facing the street.

At the next shop, I asked for chai (tea) and kofe (coffee). A similar-looking guy as the first kiosk behind the little glass window showed me a big bottle of instant Nescafe. I did not have enough money and went to the third shop and saw through the window the instant Nescafe coffee packets. I wanted one packet, but the face in the small window insisted that I buy two, so I did. I just wanted to be back in my apartment.

Navigating my way through the front door and the dark hallway, I returned to the apartment to enjoy my still-hot bread. I boiled some water to make the instant coffee. At about 11:00 a.m., someone rang my doorbell. I loudly said in English that I do not speak Russian. The banging continued. Through the peephole, I saw an angry man trying to tell me something, and finally, with a gesture of giving up, he turned off the switch to my hallway lights. I heard something like tratit, which I looked up in my dictionary as "waste." Apparently, he was telling me that I was wasting electricity. I was told in my welcome folder that a teacher was already assigned to start intensive Russian lessons eight hours a day five days a week on Monday for three months. After which, I would start my work as the regional health officer to manage the restructuring and reforms of the healthcare system in the region.

By the time I unpacked my bags, it was afternoon, the sun was bright, and the temperature was in the high 60s. I took out my Almaty map and went for a walk. I wanted a better view of the Altai range. My map showed that I was two blocks from the Almaty concert hall, four blocks from Panfilov Park, where the Ascension Cathedral is located, which is famous for its wood structure built without a single nail. I walked to the park, went in the church, and lit a candle for no one in particular. I sat on one of the pews and reflected upon the last twenty-four hours and the newness of my surroundings, with some trepidation and excitement at being in such an unknown place. That park and the church would become my retreat for the next couple of years whenever I needed a quiet place to think. The park, I discovered later, was the shortcut to walk to my work. It became my meditative walk in the morning and evening.

On my way back, the smoky aroma of grilled meat, known as shashlik, from a roadside stall went straight to my stomach, reminding me that it was time to eat. I pointed to a stick on the fire with four pieces of meat. The young Kazak with a hat, which I learned later is called a kalpak, asked me something, and I just nodded. He then took a paper plate, put a large piece of flatbread on it and then arranged the meat from the four wooden grill sticks in the middle of the bread. He sprinkled onions, tomatoes and some spices on top. He rolled the bread into a wrap and handed it to me. I mumbled what I thought was thank you in Russian. I held out some local change in my hand, hoping that I had enough left over from my morning bread and coffee. He reached out and took what I assumed was the cost for the wrap and just nodded, unsmiling, and turned to the next customer. I walked to the side of the road, sat on a bench, and enjoyed the savory flavors of my first local meal. It was a perfect way to end my first full day in Almaty. I knew at that moment that I was going to like living there and learning about a new culture and people. But first, I had to learn Russian.

My tour in Central Asia lasted from 1995–1999. Almaty was the regional USAID Mission for five Central Asian countries—Kazakhstan, Kyrgyzstan, Turkmenistan, Uzbekistan, and Tajikistan. The United States was the largest bilateral donor during that period. As part of our assistance, the regional mission provided technical assistance and resources to reform the economic, legal, banking, and social and health sectors to support the newly independent countries in their transition from state-owned economies to more market-based systems. I traveled intensively to all the offices in the other Stans, sometimes by car and sometimes by the old Russian planes, hoping that they wouldn't crash. I preferred traveling by car, if possible, despite the distance and logistical issues. I felt safer in the fleet of vehicles managed by our embassies. Plus, road travel gave me an opportunity to see the conditions in the country.

We, donors and host country counter-parts, were learning as we were implementing reforms in those early days of transition. The process of reform and restructuring from a centrally controlled system to a market-based economy was new to all of us. Much has been documented by experts about what was done right and or wrong, but for me, it was an exhilarating experience to be part of such a major reform process.

My Russian Teacher

Tatiana knocked on my door the Monday after I arrived in Almaty. The welcome kit left for me by my supervisor had all the details about when my Russian lessons would start. For three months, I was to be immersed in the Russian language with a private teacher from nine in the morning until four in the afternoon each working day. The in-country language program was an alternative to studying at the foreign language institute in the US. After three months I would be tested to see if I had achieved the minimum proficiency level in Russian. If I passed, I could come to work.

I liked Tatiana immediately. As I opened the door, her blue eyes stared at me, and she smiled and said what sounded like *doobre utro – kak ee dhela*. I assumed it meant "good morning and how are you." I just nodded, hoping she would give me instructions in English. It was not to be. I panicked a bit at the thought of eight hours without being able to understand anything she said. Part of the language training meant field trips to the market and other places, so I could be immersed in my surroundings. One such trip stands out in my memory, and I wrote a letter to Jeff about it. The section below is directly from the letter that I found in my black attaché. He must have given it back to me at some point.

Dear Jeff,

I have done two things that have improved my standing with our Kazakh staff. I used local transport and hitch-hike, just like they do. So far, I have been walking everywhere, but then there are places like the wholesale clothes bazaar (where one can buy Russian Shapkas [hats]) which is further than I want to walk. Tatiana decided that we should take the tram and tour the city and go to a different bazaar for me to shop at. My language training field trip. We took the tram No. 25 to the bazaar, and with 10 tenge in hand, I got on. The tram went down a block or so on Bagan Bayer Batir (old name Kirova)—all streets have been renamed with Kazak names of former Kazak leaders and artists. The tram then turned right on Lenina (name still unchanged). Lenina is a "bolshoi ulithsa" (big street) as it was referred to. I was able to pay for my fare when the conductor, a large woman who wore an oversized coat, big boots, showing three gold teeth, approached me. She spoke nonstop and warbled around the shaky old tram collecting money and handing out tickets. After Lenina, we turned on Abay, named after a poet, I think. We then passed the art museum and the circus arena. I believe we were headed for the flea market. I was told by Tatiana that the bazaar would be a perfect place to buy souvenirs and practice Russian. Then, we hit a truck. Just like that. We were stopped at a streetlight, and as soon as we started to move, we heard this big crash, and the army truck in front of us was pushed by our tram right off the road. Apparently, it was just parked there—I heard the driver say something in Russian, which sounded like a curse. Apparently, he had assumed that it was going to move with the rest of the traffic when the light turned green. We got off and Tatiana rushed to the next stop on the street with me trying to keep up, and we got on the next tram.

There were two aspects of this event that struck me as different. One, that it bothered no one. People just sighed, got off and walked to the next stop and got on the next tram that came or decided to go elsewhere and just walked away. What was even more interesting was the silence with which all this happened. If it was Africa or Asia, there would have been a loud discussion—arguments or advice or just sounds of amazement that more damage was not done, and crowds of people would have gathered to just see what happened. In this case, I was struck by the quietness with which everyone scattered away in different directions or got on the next tram. I, of course, wanted to wait and look to see what would happen next, but my teacher kept me moving on. We had to get to the bazaar. We finally made it to the bazaar, which was so crowded I could not believe that there were so many people living in Almaty. Everyone pushed and shoved to get by. No "excuse me" here. I bought a Shapka. I got to ask, "*Skolka eto Stoyit*?" (How much does it cost?) over and over at every shop. The return trip was uneventful. Tatiana got off at one of the stops on the way back as it was close to four in the afternoon and the end of my class. I got off with her. I was not ready to go home yet. I started walking toward the direction the bus was headed. But realized that I was too far from the house, so I hitched a ride. I have by now mastered how to say the name of my street and the cross street correctly in Russia, but I also carry a piece of paper to show to the drive if they do not understand me.

More tomorrow, love.

I learned much from Tatiana about the old times and the new changes. Some days after the class was over, I would ask her questions in English about her life under the Soviet system. She told me that it had been difficult in Kazakhstan for most of the people and was like a double-edged sword. On the one hand, she said that being free from suspicion and oppression was something people were happy about, that they didn't have to worry about who was telling what about them or someone making up something about them that could send them to jail forever. "We don't have to live and sleep and eat in fear all the time anymore, and that is a good thing. But the new system is also confusing. No one knows the rules except those in power. In the old days we knew if we worked for so many years, we would get an apartment, and a dacha (summer house in the country), then after some years, a car was allotted, and holidays were a sure thing. We knew we always had shelter and food. Not anymore. Everyone is out for themselves."

Tatiana took me to her house as part of my lessons to meet and see how ordinary people lived. She introduced me to Russian food, borscht, verenki, beetroot salad, and more. I never really developed a taste for borscht which is many people's favorite. She lived in a one-bedroom apartment with her mother, her sister and her sister's two children. The living room turned into the dining room during meals and a bedroom at night for the kids. The apartment was allotted to her by the government, which she was able to buy after independence.

My intensive language training ended after three months. I had passed the minimum level required for my job. I was both frustrated and fascinated by the complexities of the Russian language. I wanted to master it more than I did in three months, as I wanted to be able to talk and learn about the people I was working with. I continued my lessons for an hour twice a week throughout my stay in

Almaty. I wanted to be able to read Pushkin and other Russian writers. I only succeeded in reading simple children's books by the time I completed my tour in 1999.

I regret that I lost touch with Tatiana. When I visited Almaty again in 2016, I tried to find her but was not successful. She was my first contact with a country I knew so little about. My lack of Russian and her unwillingness to speak openly about her life, even in English, made it difficult for me to ask the many questions that I had. Sometimes, I felt that the lifelong habit of being cautious about what one says got in her way. I can still visualize her sitting across the table from me and not giving in when, in frustration, I would speak English to get clarification, and she would look at me like she did not understand what I was saying until I found a word in Russian. As hard as those three months were, I had looked forward to my lessons each morning with Tatiana. I had started to fall in love with the Russian language.

I also discovered that in addition to assuming that all Americans are evil from the propaganda films shown during the Soviet Union times, Americans were also spies and not to be trusted. However, old Bollywood movies from the 1950s were popular in the region, and I would often be asked when walking in the park or just walking, if I knew Raj Kapoor, the famous Indian movie star of the fifties. I thought it was my Indian heritage that made me a bit less of a suspicious person. Even then, it took more than a year before my neighbors in the building would greet me and look me in the eye and say "*Drastivityia*," the Russian greeting.

Landing in Armenia

My landing in Yerevan, Armenia, was less eventful as compared to Almaty and Ouagadougou. I was, by then, a seasoned foreign service officer. Yerevan was my third tour, and with some Russian in my vocabulary, I could navigate my way around a bit better and with less trepidations.

The people of Armenia won my heart for their hospitality and kindness. During my first tour in Armenia from 1999 to 2001, Jeff and I would take trips on weekends to see the churches and historic sites. One trip is marked in my memory as a constant reminder of the warmth of the Armenian people. We had heard by word of mouth that Aghavandzor, a village southeast of Yerevan, had prehistoric stone structures and an old church located on a hill near the village.

On one Saturday, we took our new SUV and headed towards the village. Reaching the foothill where the village was located, we stopped to ask a shepherd boy, who was about twelve years old, for directions. He shook his head and then cupped his hands over his mouth and, facing the next hill, started a message in a song-like manner in Armenian. We could see no one in the distance. The hill he faced was scattered with grazing sheep. Then we heard a high-pitched voice floating across the hill. The young shepherd turned to us and, in broken Russian, told us to go straight, then turn left, then cross a small stream, get to the village, find the teacher, Amin, who will lead us to the church.

Finding the teacher's house was not a problem once we reached the village. Everyone knew the local teacher. Amin opened the door and before we could say a word invited us into the courtyard as if he was expecting us. I was wondering if one of the shepherd boys had run to the village in advance to give the teacher a heads-up. He led us to the courtyard and requested that we sit on a wooden bench under the shade of the surrounding grapevines. A long table in front of the bench was soon covered with grapes, homemade cheese, homemade wine, and black olives, along with lavash, the thin Armenian bread, most likely made by the teacher's mother, who joined us. She looked so happy to see us and talked away in Armenian. We understood no word of what she said. Her son tried to translate into Russian. After the mother was satisfied that we had eaten and had enough wine, the teacher accompanied us to the site we were in search of. Another five miles on a rough path, barely drivable, stood the small church on top of a small hill next to a large tree. We knew that there were old stones scattered around, and we all went in different directions to find them. We saw two five-foot stone pieces which stood upright with markings of snakes, a bird and other animals that had been eroded with age. These stones are called dragon stones, or vishaps, and are found in the highlands of Armenia. The exact period of their construction is unknown and is estimated to be between 4,000 to 7,000 years ago, depending on the region.

After spending a short meditative time on the hill, we headed back. Amin accompanied us until we reached the main road back to Yerevan. His mother had packed a small basket of more lavash and cheese for us in case we got lost on our way home.

This was not the only time that I experienced such extreme hospitality. I met with similar hospitality on most trips whenever we stopped to ask for directions. Such openness to the Armenian homes took some getting used to, even for me, who grew up in Punjab, where people have a reputation for being friendly.

I served in Armenia from 1999–2001 and then again from 2009–2012. One day, I hope to write about my work experience in a country and people so rich in history and resilience. Whenever I get a message from a friend, it invokes an image of lavash, cheese, wine, and fruits of all kinds, especially grapes, spread out in front of me on a table by a grandmother, a mother or a sister, total strangers, but so welcoming at heart.

The Blue Skies of Asmara

It is September of 2004, and I am working and living in Asmara, capital of Eritrea, on a plateau on the northwest side of the African Rift Valley, at the height of over six thousand feet. Between 1936–1941, under Italian rule, Asmara underwent an architectural transformation with a blend of European art-deco buildings within a North African culture, creating a visually awe-inspiring urban setting. Asmara's climate is a delight. Its crystal-clear blue skies, with moderate temperatures in the mid-seventies, make it perfect for tennis and walking all year round.

It is Friday the 24th around 7:00 p.m. My mother is visiting from India. I am in the kitchen. My house, constructed in the early 1940s, is typical of the villas designed for Italian immigrants under colonial rule. It is a four-story house between two streets and surrounded by a stone wall. The entrance to the garage is from the lowest street level.

There is a small gate with fifteen steps leading to a large garden artistically maintained with seasonal flowers and a magnolia tree in the middle. There is a picnic table with chairs that we often use for lunches and evening get-togethers. From the garden, another set of steps leads to a small balcony that overlooks the lovely garden and the Asmara hills and blue sky. This balcony is the official entrance to the house, but I seldom use it. A second entrance, which I do use, is from the uppermost street, which has a large steel gate that opens into the driveway. There is another garden surrounding the upper floor of the house, the kitchen, the dining room, and the living room. The kitchen door is right off the driveway, a much easier way to enter the house. It is not a convenient house but is architecturally interesting, with different levels of gardens and entrances and greenery.

On this evening, I am standing by the window with a glass of wine in my hand, watching my mother puttering outside in the garden. The evening sun casts shadows and highlights the colors of the red earth, filling the kitchen with warmth. As I watch her, I am filled with happiness and gratitude for her good health at the age of eighty-one. My younger sister is planning to visit from Berkeley in October. All three of us have made plans to travel around the country, enjoying each other's company and taking walks under the clear blue skies of Asmara.

I am pouring a glass of water to take to my mother, as she has been out in the sun for some time when the phone rings in the hallway. From the window, I see my mother putting away the tools, dusting her hands and walking towards the kitchen door. I am content. My mom is with me. My sister will be with me shortly. I casually lift the receiver and say, "hello." I am jolted by the sound of my sister sobbing at the other end of the line.

"I went to wake him up, and I knew he was no more and that he was dead. I have been so worried about him doing something like this. I was a good mother." I hear her say. I suddenly feel very cold. A chill like I have never experienced before takes hold of my body, and a heavy silence descends upon the house like blackness. There is a silence so deep that I can hardly breathe. The fading sunlight, so peaceful a half-hour ago, casts a dark, frightening shadow across the room. I hear my sister's voice, which seems so far away. "I can't call anyone. You take care of it. I can't talk to Mom right now." She hangs up. I slowly put the phone down.

I turn to my mother, who by now is standing by me. I hug her. "He is no more, he died." We stand there holding each other in complete stillness. We do not know what else to do. After what seems like an eternity, I say, "We need to make calls." I call my brother, who lives in India, and set in motion the mundane process of logistical arrangements and travel plans across three continents.

My mom stopped eating or talking for long enough that I became worried. "What's the point?" she asks. She ages with each passing day. Her cheeks grow hollow, and her eyes grow sadder. She cannot bring herself to talk to my sister when I suggest that she should.

"What is there to say?" she says. Her heart is broken at the loss of her only grandson.

My sister and I agreed during one of our conversations that it would be better for mom to stay in Asmara. My sister says that she will visit as planned in October. "Instead of traveling and relaxing for fun, we can grieve together." My heart stops, hearing the grief in her voice.

In October, when my sister comes to Asmara, we talk and talk about my nephew in the hope that talking will bring some relief to me.

We take long walks under the clear blue skies hoping the rhythm of our steps together will make me forget that he is no more. We go to Massawa, the old port, and I soak my heavy heart in the warm salty waters of the Red Sea, hoping that it will wash my grief away. We look at the family photo albums. I laugh and cry and share stories, hoping to re-live his life to help me live mine. Mornings and nights merge into one, and I move through the motions of living but not living.

Then, one day it was time for my sister to leave. We have our moment together, sitting in the garden over a cup of tea before she leaves for the airport. I looked around the garden my mom so meticulously worked on when she arrived, but I hardly noticed the new blooms. The sky is the same as always, crystal clear and blue, but I see it not. I sit with my sister and have nothing to say. We hug each other. We put her bag in the car. She spends a quiet moment with Mom. She gets in the car, and we drive off under the clear blue skies.

"I am glad you came," I say. I want to say more but cannot. What is there to say? I knew, then, deep in my heart, that grief had come to live with me and that these moments are just the beginning of a lifetime of grieving for my only nephew. I love him very much.

Simmering Onions

One fall morning in Madison, I found myself standing at the kitchen counter gazing from the window at the maple tree, which had started to change colors from green to red. I had invited some good friends for a casual dinner and was pondering about what to do next. I am not a good cook, nor do I like cooking. What was I thinking? However, the vegetables and the meat were out of the refrigerator waiting to be added to the onions in the red Le Creuset pot. As I started to chop the vegetables, the smell of the simmering onions carried me back to a memory of my mother's traditional India kitchen in 1945.

I am a toddler, maybe three years old, sitting on the ground next to my mother, who is sitting on a low stool chopping vegetables for the evening meal. It is still daylight. A stainless-steel pot on a handmade earthen stove, rectangular in shape with the front open for feeding wood and coals, is ready to receive the vegetables. I pick some vegetables, possibly carrots and potatoes, and throw them on the floor. She ignores me first, and I keep doing it again and again, making a game of it. She loses patience and asks me to stop. I pay no attention. She then commands me to stop throwing the vegetables on the ground in the voice she uses to discipline our puppy. I continue, slyly watching her reactions. Finally, she shrugs and calls Inder Singh, who worked at the agriculture extension farm my father was employed at and happened to be around to take me away from the kitchen.

Inder Singh picks me up and carries me to the shed where his cargo farm bike with a huge wheelbarrow full of hay is parked. He places me on the hay. He mounts the bike, and off we go riding around the farm through the wheat fields. He is humming a local Punjabi song that I do not understand, but I like the sound of his voice. He points out the rice, maize and other crops that are waiting to be harvested. We ride around the bare plowed fields made ready for the wheat to be planted. There are fruit trees, mangoes, ripe and ready to be eaten. I feel my hair flying in the air. I want to sing along with Inder Singh. I laugh and laugh with pure happiness, and I feel light and free.

The smell of the simmering onions, softened and caramelized to dark brown, nearly burnt, brought me back to my kitchen and to the fall morning in Madison. I looked again out the window at the brilliant red maple tree next to the yellow American elm, and I wanted to be outdoors. I felt a longing for the pure sensation of joy that I felt as a child. Cooking will just have to wait, I said to myself aloud. My friends will have to understand. I set down the knife. I turned off the stove. I put the meat in the refrigerator. I put on my walking shoes and walked outside. I headed towards Lake Monona.

At the lake, I sat on a bench and was immersed in the breeze. I watched the boats and the kayaks in the distance and let my spirit float with them as they got further and further away. I wanted to be one of those boats. I wanted to float away. I closed my eyes to relive the joy that I felt being outdoors as a child in that faraway place so long ago. Inder Singh's voice sounded in my head, a song that sounded familiar and soothing. I did not remember the words. I am not sure if I imagined this memory. I was three years old, but the memory lives as if it was real, and it made me feel calm. I got up from the bench and headed home. I had to deal with the simmering onions, but I was ready and looking forward to seeing my friends.

Let's Have Tea

In December 2021, I went to see my ninety-seven-year-old mother, who lives in Chandigarh, located in the foothills of the Indian Himalayas. During the day, we sat in the family room with not much to do or places to go, thanks to COVID. The room, where my mother usually positions herself with her knitting paraphernalia, is the center of the house from where she can stay in touch with what is going on and who is doing what. It helps her stay connected. It is also the place where friends and relatives who visit sit. These visits are usually pronged by moments of silence, having covered the basic small talk. During these lapses, someone will say, "let's have tea." Having tea is India's favorite time filler.

My mother has lived in many houses, and my nieces and nephews have grown up, yet nothing seems to change when I hear that sentence, "let's have tea." It takes me back every time to the many visits and many cups of tea with family. This is no ordinary tea where you boil the water, find a tea bag, put it in a cup, pour the water over it, let it soak, take out the tea bag, add sugar and milk, and there, the tea is ready. However, "let's have tea" is special. The water is boiled in a small pan, a spoon of tea leaves, most likely from the region of Assam, are dropped in the water, followed by cinnamon, cardamon, and one clove—no more than one. The water comes to a boil, milk and sugar are added, one more boil and the tea is ready. Ginger is an option. Cups are lined up on the tray, and the tea is strained into them, steaming of wonderful spicy aroma.

My memory of the tea ritual goes back to my childhood in India. Everyone was always sitting around and drinking tea. I often wondered if no one had any work to do. I soon discovered that it was a family pastime. I used to think that it was such a waste of time. But when I first came to the States and often was lonely. I would take out a pan and do the whole process of making hot spicy tea. I made it the Indian style. I had a special pot labeled "for tea making only."

No one could use it for any other purpose. I would put the pot on the stove and wait for the water to boil. I would then add tea leaves from the Indian Assam hills, where tea is grown and was available at the Indian store in Ann Arbor. I would then add milk, sugar, lots of it, cinnamon, and occasionally a clove. I would pour it into a cup and carry it with me while I got dressed. The aroma of spices and tea made me feel at home, and the long winter months were a bit more bearable. Over the years and after throwing out many pots which had darkened with acidity from the tea leaves, or were difficult to clean in a dish washer, I finally changed to tea bags for convenience, but then there are times when I hear that voice—lets have tea —and I find a pan that I take out and make tea the old fashioned way.

During my visits to India, I often spend time with my mother before she goes to sleep. We play cards, and other times we just talk about the past and how things were, and sometimes she wants to talk about the future. She is ninety-eight years old, and she has plans. Sometimes during our chat, she says, "let's have tea. You want tea?" We go to the kitchen and make it the special way. We bring our two steaming hot mugs to her bedroom. We hold our mugs tightly between our two hands and continue our chat while sipping hot Indian tea. It all feels so right.

My Niece in Ghana

In hot and humid Ghana
where birds do not stir
stretching her arms as if newly awakened
she steps onto the verandah
and walks to the sofa.

On which, she lazily reclines.
She ponders her next move.
With a mirror in her hand
she plucks unwanted eyebrow hair
she tends to her nails
wondering what color fits her mood.

Her body plunges deeper in the sofa
as if the sofa was a soft wrapper.
While she twirls her long black hair
"Should I get braids, should I not?" she asks.
Then, she looks at me and says,
"Do you think I am being too self-indulgent?"

The phone rings, making me jump.

A timeless moment.
Then off she goes
chatting and giggling
to the voice on the other end.
Making evening plans.

I watch the soft spot where she sat
feeling the warmth
of space she left behind.
Will she return and be the child
I want her to be...
The child that I never had.

My Grandniece on Willy Street

Wearing her bright pink jacket
her red shoes still untied.
She is restless to walk
down Willy Street.

She tugs my hand, insisting.
Her big brown eyes
looking at me, she blurts
"I want walk Willy Street."
She is three years old.

We come to St. Vinny's.
She runs around excited.
Among discarded memories
she finds a Nemo puzzle.
Like a treasure
She puts it in her pocket.

We walk to Cargo bike.
She points to a red bike
"That is MY favorite"

"Can I, have it?"
I shake my head, fearing a pout
but we move on
down Willy Street.

We approach Few Street
space opens to tall trees.
"My Orton Park," she excitedly yells.
We walk to the swings
her face lights up.

I slide her in the kiddy swing
her hair blowing in the wind
"Higher, higher" she sings.

It's time to leave, she turns to wave
"Bye,Bye Orton Park"
"Ice cream? She tugs my hand again.

She has been away for six months
I missed her much.
I was afraid that she would not know me,
my fears were unfounded.

Finding My Space in Madison

Moving to Madison was hard. I left Washington, DC, in 1985 for my first international job after postgraduate work in Ann Arbor; when I returned to the US in 2012, I had not made a home there since 1985. When working overseas, I was used to being in the limelight. I was used to being the chief guest at events and giving opening speeches and speaking to the media. I was accustomed to interacting with high-level colleagues from different countries. I was used to managing and overseeing large amounts of US government resources. I was used to an intensively busy work structure even with no set hours. I was recognized by my agency with seven superior and meritorious awards for my work, mostly in hardship posts. I thrived on the fact that I could always be on call when needed and relied upon to get the job done. As one of my colleagues said, "Do you ever sleep?" And another said, "We never worked so hard and had so much fun doing it." I considered myself lucky to have found a job that I was passionate about and loved doing it. I felt that my life and what I did had a purpose. But I was not prepared well for my retirement in Madison.

Madison, and the neighborhood we moved into, was not a particularly welcoming place for me in the beginning. Most families had lived in the neighborhood for a long time and had formed close-knit groups. I was lost in the neighborhood. Jeffrey's family and his friends made me feel at home and were always there for me. But that was not enough. I wanted my own territory, purpose, and space if Madison was going to become my home. I knew that I wanted to do something that would engage people, but I did not want a full-time teaching job in international work. I wanted to do something different. I started dreaming about having a place of my own where I could hold discussions and invite people to give talks or just get together to talk about issues that mattered to them and the community, much like a salon. I wanted to engage, and engage others, in the art of conversation.

In early 2012, I bought a building that felt just right. Located on Williamson Street, two blocks from the condo we had moved into, it was part of the historical buildings on Williamson Street. It was built in 1896 for Frank G. Dickert, who operated a shoe shop and lived next door. The place felt perfect for my vision of a salon. I finished the renovations by November and called it "A Place to Be." It became my place to be.

Then, in September of 2012, at the Willy Street Fair, I was volunteering to register voters when a young man came up to me and said, "I want you to join the Marquette Neighborhood Association Board. I am going to be running for the board myself." His invitation took me by surprise, and I said, "I would love to, but no one knows me. Who will vote for me?" He said that I should leave that to him. Later, I found out that he was a strong advocate for the neighborhood and excellent at networking. I did follow up on his invitation and wrote up a short paragraph to demonstrate why I would be a good candidate to advocate for the neighborhood. I was a little embarrassed writing up the justification. I had never done any work in local communities before, and my international experience was not well understood by most people in the neighborhood as I was often asked what USAID stood for and did. But on election day, to my surprise, I was elected to be on the board. I was totally surprised by being elected by people who hardly knew me. Maybe they wanted a fresh face on the board. Whatever the reason, being on the board and working on local issues helped me connect with people, make my own friends, and give back to the community. I felt I had found a purpose. That first step led me to join other community and business boards, which further expanded my presence in the community. It felt good to be working on local development issues after spending so much of my life overseas and dealing with the development of other countries.

That first winter of 2012, I also joined a Zumba class. I had taken some classes in Armenia and loved it. I was thrilled to discover that a class was offered two blocks from the condo. I enrolled. I nearly walked out of the first class as everyone looked so fit and so young. But I said to myself, "I am here to exercise and to meet people." The teacher, young in appearance, looked like one of the fit instructors on YouTube. I loved her energy and how she made all of us, young and old, feel we could all Zumba. For two years or more, we became a family, dancing to Latin rhythms twice a week. The Zumba instructor remains a close friend and plans to walk with me around Lake Monona to celebrate my eightieth birthday.

Then there is my Friday tennis group. I started playing tennis when I first went overseas in 1985. Growing up, I played badminton and later squash, so tennis was new, but I fell in love with it in Bangladesh the first time I hit a ball with my new Yonex racket. Jeff and I joined the Cherokee Golf and Tennis Club on the east side of Madison. The drive through the quiet neighborhoods was perfectly calming for me before playing. Plus, I could reserve the courts for more than an hour. The lounge at the club won me over as I could meet people for drinks and socialize after our matches. Over the years, a small group of five women from a league of twenty-five or more wonderful ladies and no-nonsense tennis players started playing on Fridays. A librarian, an artist, an administrator, a retired FedEx manager, and me, the diplomat. We five women, very different in age, backgrounds, and professions, bonded together through tennis. Over time, we have formed a social group for outings, dinners, and to just hang out together. They have become my own go-to group for fun, support and encouragement.

I can think of many other situations where a person reached out to me when I needed it most. But it took effort on my part to put myself out there, which was not easy at the age of seventy. When I first opened A place to Be, I walked to all the small businesses on Willy Street, many of which were owned and managed by women. We formed an informal women's business network. We met once a month at first and then over time less frequently once the network was operational. I met many remarkable women who have become friends over time through that business network. I was impressed at their resilience—many of them were single moms with young kids. They believed in their entrepreneurship. I felt humbled listening to their experiences in making a success of their businesses.

I have lived on Madison's east side since 2012, a neighborhood known for its progressiveness. It has not always been easy. But finally, I do feel that I fit in.

Lake Miner in September

Gud woke up at dawn and looked out of the window. The sun rays simmered on the still water of Lake Miner, one of the Chain O Lakes in Waupaca, Wisconsin. She put on her shoes and went out for a walk through the foggy early morning mist, down a narrow gravel driveway lined with pine trees to the main road. It was a chilly September morning, and she realized she needed something warmer than her T-shirt. She returned to the cabin and found her fleece jacket in the bedroom closet. Her husband, Jeffrey, was softly snoring under the comfort of a blanket. Gud went to the kitchen and put some water on the stove for tea. She chose a large mug from the shelf and added the PG Tips tea bag, sugar, and milk, before pouring the hot water into the mug. She carried her tea out to the pier and sat on one of the white chairs placed to view the expansive landscape.

Gud wrapped both hands around the mug while sipping her tea for a little warmth. Her gaze followed to where the blue lake merged with the sky, separated by the tree line shadows, creating a Monet-like picture. A man in a kayak moved into her view, with a fishing rod perched in front, steadily working his way, searching for a perfect place to stop, and cast. She looked towards the other shore and saw a pontoon boat come through a narrow channel from the connected lake "wake to no wake" waters. The boat leisurely moved towards the cabin. She heard voices:

He: "We should buy a house on the lake."

She: "We will never be able to afford one, let us just have a kid instead."

They were unaware of how the sound carried over the lake. Gud at one time also wanted to have kids. She knew she could not have children of her own, a genetic condition, but adoption could have been an option. Why had she not, she wondered? Many of her friends had adopted, maybe she would be less lonely now, if she had.

There was not much activity on the lake as the summer season was over. The kayak moved towards her side of the lake and then silently changed direction towards the next cottage. The person in the kayak was toying with the fishing rod and made a choice that the water near the next cottage looked better for fishing. Gud thought of all the choices she had made in life. Some were well thought out, and some were just because there had been no other choice, or so she thought.

Gud always wanted to have a career. Her father went to the US when she about twelve years old to get his PhD from Cornell University. Watching his PANAM two propeller plane take off from the Delhi airport, she decided to herself that she would do the same when she grew up.

After finishing high school, she decided to enroll in the pre-med program. She soon realized that she hated dissecting animals. She shifted to psychology. The heavy focus on Freud's school of psychotherapy, which was in vogue at that time, disillusioned her. She could not see its usefulness, especially in India. She found it condescending towards women. She changed her major to sociology. She knew she wanted to have a profession where she could help people and make the world a better place. After graduation and not knowing how to get to her career path, she decided to go to a typing school in Delhi and worked as a secretary in the Ford Foundation, Delhi office. Ford Foundation had programs in health and agriculture, and she hoped that the exposure to these programs might help her make a career choice.

During this time, her aunts and extended aunties had started to make comments to her mother, such as, "she is at the right age to get married and get settled." To them, being a secretary was wasting time. But marriage was not an option for Gud. She wanted to work and be independent before she got married. She reviewed all her options and chose social work and enrolled in the Delhi School of Social Work. She had not forgotten about her dream to go to the US for her PhD, just like her dad. She had to figure out how to find the resources to get there. Her father, as a civil service officer, could not afford the tuition and living expenses. She needed a scholarship.

As part of her social work program, Gud was assigned to a slum area in Delhi. She worked with a professor from California who had a doctorate in public health. She saw him working with the policymakers and the communities to help with policies and implementation practices. She decided that she wanted to work in the public health field. The professor, who became her mentor, helped her apply to the Johns Hopkins School of Public Health. Six months later, when she was giving up hope, she received a letter from John Hopkins saying that she was admitted to the Doctor of Public Health program with a full scholarship and a stipend for living expenses. She had to get there by August of 1969. She had a year to prepare. While sipping her tea on the shores of Lake Miner, Gud could still feel the sense of elation and freedom that she felt then at receiving the letter.

Meanwhile, Jeffrey had woken up and had put a kayak in the water from the second pier, which was behind the cabin. The cabin was built on a peninsular with water surrounding its three sides. It has two piers hidden from each other with pine trees. Gud did not see him until he came around to her side of the cabin. He said he would be back in a couple of hours. He had his fishing gear with him. She had the whole morning to herself, she thought. She went into the cabin and made another cup of tea. She wanted to write. She walked to the living room and took her journal out of her backpack. Gud had been keeping a journal for years. She had not given much thought as to what she would do with her journal entries. But she kept a journal because she felt she needed to write.

Gud was twenty-six years old in the summer of 1968 when she got the news about her admission to John Hopkins. The timing was perfect as social pressure to get married was mounting from the aunties, who would say, "Who are you waiting for?" "No one is perfect," or "You do not want to be a single woman when you get old in India." "You can always finish your PhD after you get married. Nothing is stopping you from doing both." At times, she felt weakened in her resolve and started to wonder why she could not do both.

While she was in the school of social work, she met John, who worked for an international organization. For two years, they talked about a life together, and she could see herself doing both—marriage and a career. The relationship ended when John announced that he wanted to meet someone else who could have his children. John knew that Gud could not have children but had never mentioned that it was an important issue for him. What a coward, Gud thought. But she was devastated. She let her life collapse around her. August came and passed. She did not get on the plane to go to Baltimore. She was determined to make a course correction, which was not such a good idea in her mental state. She chose the wrong course correction, she got married to someone else on the rebound. She married Tim, who had expressed interest in dating Gud for some time. Now that Gud was not with John, Tim proposed. She said yes. She thought she had no options.

Tim was finishing his tour with his organization and knowing that they would live in the US at some point since Tim was from there, Gud initiated her immigration application. It was during the first months of her marriage when Gud realized that Tim was a player. Gud had no skills or resources to deal with the situation.

Three years into the open marriage that she had not bought into, Gud packed two bags and left Tim. She flew to New York, where her best friend, Karen, lived. Gud felt old at the age of thirty and emotionally drained and physically exhausted by the time she reached New York. Gud did not tell her parents. How could she explain to them that she had made such a life-changing mistake? She also did not want to be pitied by the aunties. She did not want her parents to be put in a position to explain her mistakes. Going to India and being with her family would have been easy and comforting, but first, she wanted to get her life back on track. She applied to several public health programs. In June of 1975, at the age of thirty-three, she got accepted to the School of Public Health in Ann Arbor, Michigan, with a full scholarship and living expenses. She moved to Ann Arbor in August 1975.

Gud was back on track to get her PhD in the US. She put in the divorce papers and changed her name back to her maiden name. She was a US citizen by then. She had the resources to finish her degree. All she saw in the future were endless opportunities and freedom. She was finally on the right road, despite some wrong turns.

Gud looked up from her journal and saw Jeffrey's yellow kayak emerging from the shadows at the far end of the lake. Gud closed her journal, got up from the chair and took her teacup to the kitchen. She put the journal back in the backpack. The kitchen clock read 1:00 p.m. She took two beers out of the refrigerator. She walked out of the cottage. Jeffrey waved as he saw her coming out of the shadows of the pine trees that surrounded the cottage. She waved back and walked to help him dock his kayak.

My Pandemic Story

We left Madison on March 10, 2020, for Cancun, Mexico, when the coronavirus in China had just hit the news. For eight years, Playa del Carmen had been our place to go in the winter. Jeffrey and I had spent considerable time searching for a winter getaway that met our needs and was in a similar time zone to avoid jet lag. We looked for a place where I could spend time on the beach, where we both could play tennis, do some sightseeing, people watching and enjoy good food. Playa Del Carmen met our criteria.

I felt comfortable taking the trip. I had plenty of practice living in disease-prone countries in Africa and Asia during my career. But once we got to Playa, news about the virus in the US seemed to get worse. We heard about a shortage of hospital beds, sick people in ambulances waiting for beds in ICU's, shortages of ventilators and exponential growth in death rates. Most of the US, including Madison, was starting lockdown procedures. From a distance, it was hard to believe that this was happening in America.

Life in Playa appeared normal, with tourists still on the beaches and businesses and restaurants open. But each day, the city got emptier and quieter, and there was talk of a lockdown. There was news about reduced flights, and some airlines had stopped operating flights to Mexico. Countries in Latin America had started to close their borders. Our hotel, we heard, might shut down if the lockdown was announced in Playa. We began to worry about being stranded in Mexico. We decided to cut short our trip and return home. I called American Airlines and was able to change our return tickets. The gravity of the situation hit me when we got in our taxi, and the hotel manager shut the main gate behind us. The taxi driver informed us that a lockdown had been ordered. We were the last guests to leave the hotel.

When we got to the airport, the few passengers silently wandering around in the half-closed airport appeared lost without the hustle and bustle of restaurants and shops. Our flight was on time, but when it landed, no one got off the plane, and right away, boarding was announced. American Airlines had flown an empty plane to bring us home, like in an evacuation. There were thirty-three passengers who boarded the plane for Chicago. No one talked or coughed or sneezed. Masks were not a requirement yet. It was an incredibly ghostly flight. I did not know what to expect on landing. The quietness that greeted us as we disembarked at the O'Hare International Airport was unnerving. With military-style efficiency, we were guided out of the international terminal and were waiting to board our flight for Madison at the domestic terminal in record time.

During the three weeks that we were away, a new order of social behavior had been established in Madison. We could go out for brief periods to exercise and to get essential items such as food and medicines. After my required period of quarantine, I ventured out for walks. I was surprised to see people, who are usually friendly in the Midwest way, looking away as I approached them, some even jumping aside if they thought that I was too close. Some of our friends decided to move to the country for complete isolation. In fear and uncertainty, everyone was figuring out how to live under lockdown.

Jeffrey and I tried to stay positive. I was the family cheerleader with slogans like "this will pass," "we are in it together," "we will get through this," "this is a great opportunity to catch up on our reading and household projects that have been pending." "If you can't see family and friends, call them more often, take advantage of the time you have on your hands while in isolation." And on and on. These words slowly faded away and sounded hollow as the pandemic prolonged. I had lived in many countries where I did not speak the language, had few friends, and felt fully prepared to deal with any social isolation. Until I was not. Walking one day on State Street during the lockdown, it felt surreal, like a Hollywood studio set, complete with banks, museums, shops, and restaurants all empty and dark. I wanted to shout "AND ACTION" wanting the cameras to roll and people to show up. I felt like the world had come to a stop. I knew then that this isolation was very different than anything that I had experienced before.

As the pandemic continued, I noticed a change in myself. I started to languish. Every task could wait. Every book I wanted to read was put away—there was always tomorrow. I have time, as there is nothing else to do, I would think. My calls to friends and family became less frequent. I had nothing to say to anyone. Nothing was happening except for the pandemic, and I was tired of talking about the pandemic. I stopped watching the news and lost interest in TV shows and movies. I stopped work on my memoir. I worried about my family in India, especially my mother, who was ninety-six years old. I felt helpless because I could not help if something happened to her. I started to lose count of the days and dates. I started to feel mentally imprisoned.

I needed an intervention and a reset. I took up cooking as a challenge. The New York Times recipes for cookie sheet meals were perfect for me. Oil the sheet, spread out the chicken or fish, surround it with vegetables of choice, sprinkle the salt and pepper and spices. I discovered thyme, which was not even in my spice rack until then. What a difference it made to the flavor.

With more knowledge of the virus, new guidelines were available for making a safe bubble with family and trusted friends. We formed our small family bubble so I could spend more time with my niece and with my four-year-old grandniece, who lived in the same building as us. We were happy to be together. Being with my own family made me acutely aware of the burden and sorrow that grandparents and family members felt by not seeing their grandchildren. At times, I felt guilty that we could be together when others could not.

At times I would wonder what my toddler grandniece made of this pandemic and how much did she internalize the seriousness of it all. One day when she was with me, she was playing with her magnetic blocks. She organized over fifty of them into small structures and mumbled something to herself. I asked her what she was making. "I made houses, many of them." I asked who lives in the houses, and she said, "People and they cannot get out because there are germies outside all over Madison." She then reached out and started to pick up imaginary bugs and eat them, saying, "If I eat all the bugs, people then can come out."

Having a toddler around often makes you forget everything else. We focused on making her life as normal as we could. In some ways, it helped us forget about ourselves. I happily lost myself with her role-playing Cinderella and other Disney princesses. Elsa and Anna from Frozen are her all-time favorite characters. She was always Elsa and I Anna.

By early 2021, realizing that the virus might be with us for a long time, I started to redefine my life. I returned to my memoir project. Jeffrey and I started playing tennis again with a few trusted tennis colleagues, who were also very careful who they played with. We started to go out a bit more to restaurants. I started my regular phone calls to close friends and family. I found an art teacher with whom art lessons were possible, maintaining the required social distance. We thought we had found our balance within the limitations of the health guidelines. We were beginning to be content with the new normal.

Then, on January 26, 2021, Jeffrey and I were at the Cherokee Tennis Club playing doubles with a couple that we often played with. Suddenly during the second set, Jeffrey stopped. He said he hurt all over. We all stopped playing. The symptoms sounded like indigestion. Jeffrey said he would go home and take something for indigestion. Or maybe he said that he might be dehydrated. We had planned to stop for a drink with our friends after the match. My friends offered to drop me home later as Jeffrey wanted to go home then. I asked Jeffrey to text me when he got home. As I ordered my wine, I saw his text and was glad he made it home and put the phone away.

Half an hour later, we drove up to the condo. I saw two ambulances in front of our building. I rushed upstairs. Jeffrey was strapped up in a gurney, ready to be taken to the ER. Jeffrey saw me and said, "I called you," in a voice I did not recognize. The paramedic said he had a heart attack and that they had to take him to the nearest hospital. I followed the ambulance but lost my way to St. Mary's even though I knew the way. I was so disoriented at the events of the evening and what had happened. I felt angry at myself for letting him go home alone and felt guilty for having a glass of wine while he was having a heart attack. I thought of him trying to call me, and I had put my phone away. What if he had died before he was able to call 911? I was driving around frantically within the same three blocks of St. Mary's. It was 9:00 p.m. when I made it to the hospital.

The hospital staff let me see him for two minutes to collect his personal items. His glasses, his wedding ring, and a steel Sikh bracelet that my mother gave him when we got married. He never ever took it off. I could not stay and wait there because of covid restrictions. I came home. It was 11:00 p.m. I do not remember parking the car in the garage, changing out of my clothes, and getting into bed. I was in bed when after midnight, the doctor called to let me know that Jeffry's open-heart surgery was scheduled for 8:00 a.m. That night was one of the most frightening and longest nights of my life, not knowing if Jeffrey would make it or not. All the stories of people who had lost loved ones during covid but could not see or be with them flooded my mind. I could have been one of those people.

During Jeffrey's recovery period, I could not stop thinking about how I wanted to spend the rest of my life and what my priorities were. The thought that my mother, who was ninety-seven, started to haunt me, and I wanted to see her urgently. Thoughts about what could have happened to Jeffrey took hold of my dreams. I needed a reset.

By the start of 2022, the pandemic was surprisingly still with us, but it was possible to travel to more countries. We decided to go back to Mexico. We boarded the United Airlines flight to Cancun on February 7, 2022, with some trepidations. I did not know what I would find there and how careful we would need to be. As the plane took off and I ordered a Mojito to relax, I started to look forward to being warm. I wanted some quiet time on the beach to reflect. Something had shifted in me during the past two years. I wanted to understand what it was. The question of how I want to spend my next decade was something I had not thought about prior to COVID and Jeffrey's heart attack, but now it has become central. I wanted to be more mindful about how I lived my life going forward. I did not want to just live because I had to live. I was hoping that the sun and the beach would help me find some answers.

Acknowledgments

I have wanted to tell my story ever since I was young. In 2017, I started taking creative writing courses with Chris Chambers at the University of Wisconsin. His encouragement and coaching helped me make one of my life goals come true. I also thank my publisher, Ian Graham Leask and his team.

I am grateful to my friends for their thoughtful comments whenever I shared a piece with them. Particularly Dianne Tsitsos, who provided a reader's perspective on the earlier draft of the manuscript. I thank James P. Roberts, who provided a poet's perspective. To Jeffrey Wright, I say – thank you – for keeping me focused. He was always there to encourage me at times when I wanted to give up. Thank you to my family, who are happy for me and are looking forward to reading this book.

About the Author

Jantinder Cheema (nickname Gud) has lived and served in multiple countries managing and overseeing development programs. She worked in Central Asia, Armenia, South Asia, Afghanistan, and countries in Africa.

Born in 1942 in India, she witnessed history in the making as the subcontinent of India was being divided into the separate countries of India and Pakistan. As a daughter of a civil service officer, moving frequently and living in different places was an integral part of her upbringing.

In 1975, Cheema moved to the United States for graduate and post-graduate studies at the University of Michigan, Ann Arbor. After graduating, she worked with International Organizations as a development consultant and in 1991 joined the United States Agency for International Development as a career Foreign Service Officer. She reached the ranks of a Senior Foreign Service Officer before finally retiring in 2012.

During her career, Cheema sought volunteer opportunities, and participated in forums to speak to women and young professionals on leadership and career enhancement. After retirement, she founded "A Place to Be" a salon for creative conversation and dialogue, in Madison, Wisconsin, where she currently lives with her husband. She continues to actively engage in local development issues.

Cheema is passionate about writing. At A Place to Be, Cheema started working on her mother's memoir, *As I Remember – The Life History of Raminder Kaur Cheema*, which she published in association with Life History Services, LLC, in 2016. She continues to write and take coaching to become a full-time writer.

Cheema has a master's degree in Social Work, a masters in Public Health and a PhD in Social Sciences.

Made in the USA
Monee, IL
01 August 2023

40224877R00104